Civil War Librarian
96 Braddock Road
Washington, PA 15301

Copyright © 2014 by Civil War Librarian

All rights reserved. No part of this publication may be reproduced, stored in a retrieval system, or transmitted, in any form or by any means, electronic, mechanical, photocopying, recording, or otherwise without prior permission of the publisher.

All images in this book were retrieved from the Library of Congress and William H. Tipton Photographic Collection, Gettysburg National Military Park.

This book was designed by kmarie designs, Kristen Schell. Please visit www.kristenmariedesigns.com for more information.

Photo credit for the author's on the back cover: Zeb Love
www.zeblove.com | Zeb@theorganmedia.com

ISBN-13: 978-1500802349

ISBN-10: 1500802344

Volume Two
Gettysburg Campaign Study Guide
By
Rea Andrew Redd

Contents

Sections:

19. Essential Monuments: June 30, July 1 11
20. July 2: Meade Inspects His Lines and Longstreet Begins His Assault on Devils Den, Plum Run and Little Round Top 25
21. Essential Monuments: July 2 35
22. July 2: Houck's Ridge, The Stony Hill, & the Wheatfield 45
23. Essential Monuments: July 2, National Cemetery, Evergreen Cemetery 57
24. July 2: The Peach Orchard and Cemetery Ridge 67
25. Essential Monuments: July 2 79
26. July 2 4:00p to 11:00p: Ewell's Assault on Culp's Hill and East Cemetery Hill: 95
27. Essential Maps 111
28. Essential Monuments: July 2 121
29. July 2 10p to midnight July 3: 4:30a to 1:00p 130
30. July 3: The Grand Assault 143
31. July 3: Cavalry Engagement—East Cavalry Field 153
32. July 2 and 3 after 4:00p: Pennsylvania Reserves Counter Assaults 159
33. July 3, After 4p: Cavalry Engagements-- South Cavalry Field and Fairfield 165
34. Farms, Hospitals and Prisoners of War 173
35. July 4 through 14: Flight and Pursuit 189
36. The Eisenhower Farm, The George Spangler Farm, The Lutheran Seminary, Gettysburg College, Gettysburg Borough & Letterman Field Hospital 199
37. 100 More of the 175 Things Licensed Battlefield Guides Know 213
38. Essential Monuments July 2, July 2 243

Gettysburg Campaign Exam Study Guide

TO THE READER [2012]

First and foremost, the author salutes all those Pennsylvania Campaign enthusiasts who read American Civil War books, attend Gettysburg National Military Park rangers' battlewalks, subscribe to or have written for Gettysburg Magazine, are members of the Gettysburg Battlefield Preservation Association and the Gettysburg Foundation, take the Gettysburg Licensed Battlefield Guide Exam, march in or attend the Remembrance Day Parade, participate in the Adopt-A-Position Program and clean the battlefield, donate money to the Civil War Trust, participate in the Gettysburg Discussion Group on the internet, do 'living history' for the Gettysburg National Military Park, are past or present members of the Association of Licensed Gettysburg Battlefield Guides, or bring their classes and their families to the battlefield.

The American Civil War has been a lifelong interest for me. As a son, father, husband, teacher, friend, and Civil War reenactor I have been to Gettysburg countless times. I am a constant reader and have a large library that includes the three Pennsylvania Campaign volumes of the Official Records of the War of the Rebellion and quite a few of the Pennsylvania Cable Network's recordings of the battle anniversary walks hosted by the park's rangers and the licensed battlefield guides. This book presents material on the Pennsylvania Campaign in a manner that aids students of all ages and all levels of knowledge.

The material is organized in a question and answer fashion. It may be used by an individual, two people or a small group as a means of organizing their knowledge of the campaign and learning new information. The information contained herein is culled from the bibliography provided. Many of the questions have been culled from the Licensed Battlefield Guide exam offered every other even numbered year. Currently this book is the first of two volumes. Together the two volumes will have about 1,500 questions and answers on the Pennsylvania Campaign. As a work in progress, it is being offered in two volumes. This study guide format originated from hours of preparation for the exam and time spent working in an internet service known as flashcardmachine.com

As for myself, I double majored in English and history as an undergraduate and graduated 1974. I earned a master of arts in American history in 1976. I earned permanent certification as a social science instructor in the commonwealth of Pennsylvania in 1982. I earned a master of arts in library science in 1993. I have taught every grade from kindergarten through twelfth with the exception of sixth. Currently I am the director of an academic library at a Pennsylvania university and teach sections of American history there.

As a member of the Ninth Pennsylvania Reserves, I have been a Union reenactor since 1993 and have ranks of private, corporal, sergeant of infantry and captain in the medical service. I have served in both the National Regiment

[1993-2001] and Vincent's Brigade [2001-present]. I have taken the Gettysburg Licensed Battlefield Guide exam in 2006, 2008, and 2010. At first I took the exam to find out how much I knew about the Pennsylvania Campaign; now I take the exam to find how much I learned in the past two years. I offer the Gettysburg Campaign Study Guide as tool for those who seek to study the Pennsylvania Campaign for their personal enjoyment and satisfaction. At this time, I have yet to move forward to the second part of the exam that is offered in January. I wish I had these questions and answers the first time I took the exam in 2006.

Readers are welcomed to send comments and suggestions regarding the Gettysburg Campaign Study Guide to reaandrewredd@yahoo.com

>   Sincerely,

>   Rea Andrew Redd

>   http://www.civilwarlibrarian.blogspot.com

Gettysburg Campaign Exam Study Guide

TO THE READER [2014]

I wish to thank those in the U.S. and U.K. who have purchased Volume One and made it a popular book in both Gettysburg bookstores and on Amazon. com. Among the many to whom I have talked and exchanged emails, there is a common theme. The guide exam is less of a mystery after working with the book. Volume Two includes over 200 photographs of monuments and five maps of locations which are likely to appear on the test. The questions and answers cover July 2's morning through July 14.

The test is undergoing change and revision. The previous exam coordinator, Clyde Bell, passed away in 2013 and the GNMP administration is reviewing the content and frequency of offering the test. I believe that whatever form the next test takes, The Gettysburg Campaign Guide Volume One and Two contents will be applicable.

The 2012 guide exam added material that surprised test takers. The 2012 exam added material that surprised test takers, includes questions on the Eisenhower Farm, the borough, the field hospitals and civilians. Questions on the Pennsylvania Reserves during the Gettysburg Campaign are offered because Guillermo Bosch, Gettysburg Licensed Battlefield Guide, has in 2014 offered seminars and tours to The Gettysburg Foundation, private groups and individuals regarding The Pennsylvania Reserve Division and George Gordon Meade, its commander previous to Gettysburg, on the unit's actions. His research has opened up new aspects regarding strategy, tactics and combat on July 2 and July 3. Certainly, George Meade's generalship is better understood when reviewed in the light of Bosch's work.

As for myself, other projects are on the table. Currently I am editing and annotating a Fifth Corps brigade surgeon's report on his work at Chancellorsville and Gettysburg. Also, I have notes and a few drafts chapters for a book tentatively entitled Pennsylvania's Civil War: An Introduction.

Since 2012, I have travelled to the battlefields of Shiloh, Antietam, Fredericksburg, Chancellorsville, Gettysburg [of course] and Chickamauga. On the 150th anniversary of the Battle of Antietam I marched on A. P. Hill's path from Harpers Ferry to Antietam. During the 150th anniversary of the Battle of Fredericksburg I encamped and did living history on the 'Slaughter Pen' farm as well as street fighting in Fredericksburg. During 2013, I hiked on the Confederate battle lines on the crest of South Mountain and did living history on the George Spangler farm hospital at Gettysburg. In 2014, I hiked up the very steep slopes of Maryland Heights at Harpers Ferry. Within a few days of this writing and on the 150th anniversary of the Battle of Cedar Creek, I will hike up Massanutten Mountain to Gordon's observation post to view the Cedar Creek battlefield and discuss Gordon's troops route from Fisher's Hill to the the battlefield. Also, I will camp on the Cedar Creek Battlefield and participate in the reenactment. Every year for the past twelve years I have done living history with the Ninth Pennsylvania Reserves reenactment unit at the Pennsylvania Monument in the Gettysburg park.

As a student, 'living' historian and active hiker, I offer The Gettysburg Campaign Study Guide Volume Two to those who study, teach and engage the American Civil War and enjoy history. Readers are welcomed to submit comments and suggestions regarding the Gettysburg Campaign Study Guide, Volumes One and Two by sending an email to reaandrewredd@yahoo.com and visit my book news and review weblog http://www.civilwarlibrarian.blogspot.com

Sincerely,

Rea Andrew Redd

http://www.civilwarlibrarian.blogspot.com

Photographs And Maps: copyright Civil War Librarian, LLC

Photographers: Gerald C. Boehm and Rea Andrew Redd

Base Maps: Hal Jespersen, www.posix.com/CW

——— SECTION NINETEEN ———
Essential Monuments: June 30, July 1

"View south down Cemetery Ridge to the Round Tops from High Water Mark Monument. (1909s)" Tipton #2341

Gettysburg Campaign Exam Study Guide

Essential Monuments: June 30, July 1

1. First Shot Marker, Chambersburg Road west of Marsh Creek
2. Brigadier General John Buford, Chambersburg Road
3. Major General John Reynolds, Chambersburg Road

4. 149th Pennsylvania Volunteer Infantry, Chambersburg Road
5. 2nd Maine Battery, [Hall's], Chambersburg Road
6. Typical Federal Brigade Marker, Meredith Avenue

7. 150th Pennsylvania Volunteer Infantry, Buford Avenue
8. John Burns [citizen], Buford Avenue
9. 7th Wisconsin Volunteer Infantry, Meredith Avenue

Gettysburg Campaign Exam Study Guide

Essential Monuments: June 30, July 1

1. 2nd Wisconsin Volunteer Infantry, Meredith Avenue
2. 24th Michigan Volunteer Infantry, Meredith Avenue
3. 26th North Carolina Volunteer Infantry, Meredith Avenue

4. 19th Indiana Volunteer Infantry, Meredith Avenue
5. 8th New York Cavalry, Reynolds Avenue
6. Major General Abner Doubleday, Reynolds Avenue

7. 142nd Pennsylvania Volunteers, Reynolds Avenue
8. 6th Wisconsin Volunteer Infantry, Buford Avenue
9. 95th New York Volunteer Infantry, Buford Avenue

Gettysburg Campaign Exam Study Guide

1

2

3

4

5

6

7

8

9

Essential Monuments: June 30, July 1

1. 14th Brooklyn/84 New York Volunteer Infantry, Buford Avenue
2. Brigadier General James Wadsworth
3. 56th Pennsylvania, Buford Avenue

4. 6th New York Cavalry, Buford Avenue
5. 9th New York Cavalry, Buford Avenue
6. 17th Pennsylvania Cavalry, Buford Avenue

7. Peace Light Memorial, Mummasburg Road
8. 90th Pennsylvania Volunteer Infantry, Doubleday Avenue
9. 12th Massachusetts Volunteer Infantry, Double Day Avenue

Gettysburg Campaign Exam Study Guide

Essential Monuments: June 30, July 1

1. Brigadier General John Robinson, Doubleday Avenue
2. 83rd New York Volunteer Infantry, Doubleday Avenue
3. 88th Pennsylvania Volunteer Infantry, Doubleday Avenue

4. 13th Massachusetts Volunteer Infantry, Robinson Avenue
5. 11th Pennsylvania Volunteer Infantry, Doubleday Avenue
6. 94th New York Volunteer Infantry, Doubleday Avenue

7. 121st Pennsylvania Volunteer Infantry, Reynolds Avenue
8. 20th New York State Militia/80th New York Volunteer Infantry, Howard Avenue
9. 45th New York Volunteer Infantry, Howard Avenue

Gettysburg Campaign Exam Study Guide

Essential Monuments: June 30, July 1

1. 74th Pennsylvania Volunteer Infantry, Howard Avenue
2. 82nd Illinois Volunteer Infantry, Howard Avenue
3. Brigadier General Francis Barlow

4. 17th Connecticut Volunteer Infantry, Howard Avenue
5. 153rd Pennsylvania Volunteer Infantry, Howard Avenue
6. 27th Pennsylvania Volunteer Infantry, Coster Avenue

7. 154 New York Volunteer Infantry, Coster Avenue
8. 26th Pennsylvania Emergency Militia, Springs at Buford Avenues
9. Sergeant Amos Humiston and Children, Stratton Avenue

Gettysburg Campaign Exam Study Guide

Essential Monuments: June 30, July 1

1. 151st Pennsylvania Volunteer Infantry, Meredith at Reynolds Avenues
2. 143 Pennsylvania Volunteer Infantry, intersection of Chambersburg Road and Reynolds Avenue

—— SECTION TWENTY ——

July 2: Meade Inspects His Lines and Longstreet Begins His Assault on Devils Den, Plum Run, and Little Round Top

On November 29 1862 George Gordon Meade was promoted to Major General of Volunteers, and on December 25 1862 he was given command of the 5th Corps which he led at Chancellorsville. On June 28, 1863, Meade was given command of the Army of the Potomac. After the Battle of Gettysburg, he was promoted to Brigadier General in the U.S. Army [Regular] for his actions and given the thanks of Congress.

Gettysburg Campaign Exam Study Guide

QUESTIONS:

1. At what time did Meade first inspect his lines on July 2, and what was his route?

2. After his inspection, what orders did Meade give to Hancock?

3. After his inspection, what command change did Meade make?

4. After his inspection, what order did Meade give to Sickles?

5. To what location was the 12th Corps sent?

6. Around dawn which corps commander called to Meade's attention to the proximity of the Confederates to Baltimore Pike?

7. At around 10a where was the far right flank of the Federal army and which corps was there?

8. Around dawn, what orders did Henry Hunt give?

9. On the Federal right flank, what crucial gap did Hunt plug with artillery?

10. At what time did Meade order Slocum to prepare to make an assault on the Confederate left?

11. During the morning on which road did Sykes 5th Corps approach the battlefield?

12. At what time did Longstreet's July 2 infantry assault begin?

13. Which division and brigades started the assault?

14. Law's Brigade consisted of troops from which state?

15. Robertson's Brigade consisted of troops from which two states?

Meade Inspects His Lines and Longstreet Begins His Assault

Answers:

1. Beginning at approximately 2a, Meade rode from Cemetery Hill to Sickles' position and then to Culp's Hill. It is unlikely he rode to the crest of Little Round Top.

2. He ordered the 2nd Corps from the rear of Big Round Top to the Emmitsburg Road south of Cemetery Hill.

3. He placed Major General John Newton in command of the 1st Corps.

4. Sickles was to place the 3rd Corps in the location that the 12th Corps encamped on the night of July 1.

5. To Wolf's Hill and Culp's Hill

6. Slocum

7. The Federal right extended from the Baltimore Pike, across Wolf's Hill and close to the Hanover Road. The brigades of the 12th Corps were there.

8. He reorganized the artillery line on Cemetery Hill, added pieces to it, and ordered up the Artillery Reserve.

9. From lower Culp's Hill to the McAllister Mill, Hunt inserted artillery to defend the gap from lower Culp's Hill to Wolf Hill.

10. Approximately 10a

11. The Baltimore Pike

12. Between 4p and 4:30p

13. Hood's Division, Law's Brigade and Robertson's Brigade

14. Alabama

15. Three Texas regiments and one Arkansas regiment

Gettysburg Campaign Exam Study Guide

QUESTIONS:

16. Which brigades supported Law's and Robertson's brigades?

17. Under what conditions had Law's brigade reached the battlefield?

18. What caused Law's brigade to split in half and go in two directions?

19. What caused Laws to move the 44th and 48th Alabama from the right flank to the left flank?

20. After marching on the right of Law's Brigade, where did the 44th and 48th Alabama reform?

21. Which Federal troops and from what location first fired into Law's brigade?

22. After falling back from the Slyder Farm buildings, where did 2nd U.S. Sharpshooters take up another position?

23. In which directions did the 2nd U.S. Sharpshooters evacuate the summit of Big Round Top?

24. As his regiment rested on the summit of Big Round Top, what news did a courier bring to William Oates, colonel of the 15th Alabama?

25. What ANV units occupied the western slope of Big Round Top and Plum Run Valley while the 45th and 15th Alabama were near the summit?

26. At approximately what time did Vincent's Brigade occupy the summit of Little Round Top?

Answers:

16. Benning's Brigade supported Law's Brigade, and Anderson's Brigade supported Roberstson's Brigade.

17. Law's brigade had marched 28 miles in eleven hours between 2a and 1p on July 2.

18. Five companies of 47th and 48th Alabama had been advanced as skirmishers at about 3:30p; 44th and 48th Alabama that had been the brigade's right flank they were ordered by Law to move to the left flank of the brigade and ordered to attack Devil's Den.

19. The Emmitsburg Road and the path of Laws' brigade diverged; a gap grew between Law's brigade and Robertson's brigade. Law moved the 44th and 48th to his brigade's left flank in order to maintain contact with Robertson's Texas-Arkansas brigade.

20. The 44th and 48th Alabama regiments reformed on the left of Law's Brigade.

21. After firing upon Law's skirmishers, the 2nd U.S. Sharpshooters of Ward's Brigade, Birney's Division, Third Corps fired from a position west of the Slyder Farm buildings.

22. Behind a stonewall at the base of Big Round Top and after a short time among the boulders near the crest of Big Round Top.

23. Some went north and joined Company B, 20th Maine; some went south and occupied the southern face of the slope.

24. That Hood was wounded, that Law was in command of the division, that Sheffield, of the 48th Alabama, was in command of Law's brigade, and that the 15th Alabama must assault Little Round Top.

25. 4th and 48th Alabama, 4th and 5th Texas

26. Approximately 4:30p

Gettysburg Campaign Exam Study Guide

QUESTIONS:

27. List the regiments in Vincent's Brigade, from the Federal left to right, when it was finally situated on Little Round Top

28. What reasons did members of the 4th and 48th Alabama, 4th and 5th Texas give for not capturing Little Round Top's crest?

29. To what division and corps did Vincent's Brigade belong?

30. Which Federal regiment from another brigade was ordered to assist Vincent's brigade in the immediate defense of Little Round Top? From what brigade, division and corps did it come?

31. Which Federal artillery battery joined Vincent's Brigade on Little Round Top? Who commanded it?

32. Soldiers of which units assaulted the 15th Alabama as it began its withdrawal from combat with the 20th Maine?

33. Regiments of which brigade were marching north to south on the east slope of Little Round Top while the 15th Alabama was making it final assaults upon the 20th Maine?

34. By the end of the day, which elements of which two Federal brigades occupied Big Round Top and the saddle between Big Round Top and Little Round Top?

35. List the four regiments which fell in on Vincent's Brigade's right flank as Law's Brigade begans its assaults on Little Round Top. In which brigade, division and corps are these regiments?

36. Which Third Corps division sent which brigade to defend Devil's Den?

37. List the regiments in Ward's Brigade.

38. List the two AotP regiments that were later sent into the Houck's Ridge-Devils Den fight.

39. Which two AotP regiments occupied the Plum Run Valley?

Meade Inspects His Lines and Longstreet Begins His Assault

Answers:

27. 20th Maine, 83rd Pennsylvania, 44th New York, and 16th Michigan

28. Little Round Top's boulder-strewn slope broke up troop formations; exhaustion from the 28 mile march earlier that day, and the steepness of the slope.

29. 3rd Brigade [Vincent] belongs to the 1st Division [Barnes], 5th Corps [Sykes]

30. 140th New York, 3rd Brigade [Weed], 2nd Division [Ayres], 5th Corps [Sykes]

31. Battery D, 5th U.S. Lieutenant Charles Hazlett

32. Company B, 20th Maine and soldiers of the 2nd U.S. Sharpshooters

33. 9th, 10th, 11th and 12th Pennsylvania Reserves, Fisher's Brigade, Crawford's Division of the Fifth Corps

34. Fisher's Brigade of Crawford's Division and Vincent's Brigade with Colonel James Rice commanding; both brigades are units of the Fifth Corps

35. 140th and 146th New York, 91st and 155th Pennsylvania regiments, Weed's Brigade, Ayer's Division, Sykes' Corps.

36. Major General David Birney send Brigadier General Hobart Ward's brigade.

37. 20th Indiana, 3rd and 4th Maine, 86th and 124th New York

38. 6th New Jersey, 40th New York

39. 4th Maine, 40th New York

31

Gettysburg Campaign Exam Study Guide

QUESTIONS:

40. Which regiment's left flank was at the southernmost crest of Devils Den?

41. Which two ANV regiments first assaulted the crest of Devils Den?

42. As a second assault began, which Federal regiments charged down from the crest of Devil's Den?

43. Which ANV regiment fired into the left flank of the 124th New York?

44. Which two ANV regiments charged over the rocks of the Plum Run valley and overcame the 4th Maine and 40th New York?

45. Which ANV brigade supported the assault that cleared Ward's Brigade from the crest of Devils Den?

46. Which ANV regiment gained the crest of Devils Den by charging with bayonets?

47. Throughout these assaults, which Federal battery held the crest of Devils Den and then was captured?

48. Of Captain James Smith's 4th Battery of New York Light Artillery, how many were on the crest of Devils Den and how many were in Plum Run Valley?

49. During the 3rd Arkansas' first assault on Houk's Ridge, how many AotP regiments did it find on the crest?

50. As the 3rd Arkansas retreated, what did these three regiments do?

Answers:

40. 124th New York

41. 44th Alabama, 1st Texas

42. 124th New York

43. 44th Alabama

44. 44th and 48th Alabama

45. Robertson's Brigade

46. 44th Alabama

47. Captain James Smith's 4th Battery of New York Light Artillery

48. Of the 10 pound Parrott pieces, four are on the crest and two are in the valley.

49. Three regiments: 80th New York, 20th Indiana, 99th Pennsylvania

50. Charge from the crest of Houck's Ridge and caused the 3rd Arkansas to retreat further.

SECTION TWENTY-ONE
Essential Monuments: July 2

"Smith's 4th N. Y. Battery and Big Round Top," Tipton #668e (1900s)

Gettysburg Campaign Exam Study Guide

Essential Monuments: July 2

1. Typical CSA Corps Tablet, West Confederate Avenue
2. 11th Mississippi Volunteer Infantry, West Confederate Avenue
3. North Carolina State Memorial, West Confederate Avenue
4. Tennessee State Memorial, West Confederate Avenue
5. Virginia State Memorial, West Confederate Avenue
6. Florida State Memorial, West Confederate Avenue
7. 1st U. S. Sharpshooters, Company F [Vermont], Berdan Avenue
8. 1st U.S. Sharpshooters, Companies A, B, D, H, Berdan Avenue
9. Louisiana State Memorial, West Confederate Avenue

Gettysburg Campaign Exam Study Guide

Essential Monuments: July 2

1. Mississippi State Memorial, West Confederate Avenue
2. Georgia State Memorial, West Confederate Avenue
3. South Carolina State Memorial, West Confederate Avenue

4. Arkansas State Memorial, West Confederate Avenue
5. Texas State Memorial, West Confederate Avenue
6. Alabama State Memorial, West Confederate Avenue

7. Soldiers and Sailors of the Confederacy Memorial, West Confederate Avenue
8. 1st Vermont Brigade, Wright Avenue
9. 1st Vermont Cavalry Volunteer Regiment 2nd Battalion [Major William Wells], South Confederate Avenue

Gettysburg Campaign Exam Study Guide

Essential Monuments: July 2

1. 10th Pennsylvania Reserves/39th Pennsylvania Volunteer Infantry, South Confederate Avenue
2. 9th Massachusetts Volunteer Infantry, Sykes Avenue
3. 20th Maine Volunteer Infantry, Sykes and Wright Avenue

4. 140th New York Volunteer Infantry, Sykes Avenue
5. 16th Michigan Volunteer Infantry, south slope of Little Round Top
6. 12th and 44th New York Volunteer Regiments, Sykes Avenue

7. 83rd Pennsylvania Volunteer Regiment [Brigadier General Strong Vincent], Sykes Avenue
8. 91st Pennsylvania Volunteer Regiment, Sykes Avenue
9. Major General Gouverneur Warren, Sykes Avenue

Gettysburg Campaign Exam Study Guide

1

2

3

4

5

6

7

42

Essential Monuments: July 2

1. Brigadier General Samuel Crawford, Crawford Avenue
2. 63rd, 69th and 88th New York Volunteer Infantry [3/5 of Irish Brigade], Sickles Avenue
3. 10th Massachusetts Volunteer Infantry, Sedgwick Avenue
4. Father William Corby, Roman Catholic Priest, Hancock Avenue
5. Major General John Sedgwick, Sedgwick Avenue
6. New York State Auxiliary Monument, Hancock Avenue
7. 1st New Jersey Brigade Monument, Sedgwick Avenue

SECTION TWENTY-TWO
Houck's Ridge, The Stony Hill, & the Wheatfield: July 2

"From Little Round Top, looking to Devil's Den and beyond.". Same as #368
Tipton: #2758

Gettysburg Campaign Exam Study Guide

QUESTIONS:

1. What is the name of the stream over which the Confederate assault on Houck's Ridge and the Wheatfield passed?

2. Both the 3rd Arkansas and the 1st Texas assaulted the west slope of Houck's Ridge. Who was their was their brigade commander?

3. If not against Houck's Ridge, where was the remainder of Robertson's Brigade deployed at this time?

4. Brigadier General Henry Benning's brigade assaulted Houck's Ridge and Devil's Den. From which Confederate state did each of his regiments belong?

5. Who was the Federal brigade commander on Houck's Ridge and Devil's Den?

6. To whose division and corps did Ward's brigade belong?

7. Who commanded the Federal brigade that first took a position southwest of the Wheatfield?

8. Who commanded the division and corps in which de Trobriand's brigade served?

9. When Ward requested more men from Birney, which two brigades did he order to support Ward? Which regiments were sent?

10. During the retreat from the Plum Run's Slaughter Pen, which Federal regiment held the both sides of the stream?

11. Who commanded the ANV brigade that assaulted de Trobriand's position on Rose Creek?

12. From which state did Anderson's regiments come?

13. Which of de Trobriand's regiments fired into the left flank of the 3rd Arkansas as it assaulted Ward's brigade?

14. As skirmishers, which regiment did de Trobriand send to the Rose Farm buildings?

ANSWERS:

1. Rose Run

2. Brigadier General Jerome Robertson

3. The southwest slope of Little Round Top

4. Georgia

5. Brigadier General Hobart Ward

6. Major General David Birney's division of the Third Corps commanded by Major General Daniel Sickles

7. Colonel Regis de Trobriand

8. Major General David Birney's division of the Third Corps commanded by Major General Daniel Sickles

9. De Trobriand's Brigade [40th New York] and Burling's Brigade [6th New Jersey]

10. 40th New York

11. Brigadier General George Anderson

12. Georgia

13. 17th Maine

14. 3rd Michigan

Gettysburg Campaign Exam Study Guide

QUESTIONS:

15. What terrain features added to de Trobriand's defense of the Stoney Hill and the Wheatfield?

16. Birney ordered Burling to send two regiments to de Trobriand's aid. Which regiments were they?

17. Positioned in the Wheatfield, who commanded which Federal battery that supported de Trobriand's defense?

18. From another Federal corps, two brigades arrived to support de Trobriand's brigade. To what corps did these brigades belong, and who was the corps commander?

19. Who commanded the division from which two brigades were sent to aid de Trobriand?

20. State the names of the brigade commanders of Barnes' division who came to the aid of de Trobriand.

21. Where did Tilton and Sweitzer post their brigades?

22. After Anderson's brigade failed to dislodge de Trobriand's brigade, which ANV brigade assaulted de Trobriand's right flank?

23. To which ANV division and corps did Kershaw's brigade belong?

24. All of Kershaw's regiments were recruited from which state?

25. Which three of Kershaw's regiments assaulted de Trobriand's and Tilton's brigades?

26. Which three of Kershaw's regiments were distracted from the assault?

27. What Federal fire forced three of Kershaw's regiments to split away from the assault on de Trobriand's and Tilton's brigades?

28. The assault of the 3rd and 7th South Carolina struck which of Tilton's regiments?

Answers:

15. The ravine of Rose Creek and a stone wall on its northeast side.

16. 8th New Jersey and 115th Pennsylvania

17. Captain George Winslow, 1st New York Light Artillery, Battery D

18. Fifth Corps, commanded by Major General George Sykes

19. Brigadier General James Barnes

20. Colonel William Tilton and Colonel Jacob Sweitzer

21. Facing southwest and west on the west facing slope of the Stony Hill, Tilton posted his brigade behind and to the right of de Trobirand's brigade; Sweitzer posted his brigade on north end of the Stony Hill and facing northwest.

22. Brigadier General Joseph Kershaw's brigade

23. Major General Lafayette McLaws' division, Longstreet's corps

24. South Carolina

25. 3rd, 7th and 15th South Carolina

26. 2nd South Carolina, 3rd South Carolina battalion and 8th South Carolina

27. The Federal artillery stationed at the Peach Orchard

28. 118th Pennsylvania

Gettysburg Campaign Exam Study Guide

Questions:

29. During Anderson's brigade and Kershaw's brigade assaults, which Federal regiment was the only regiment actually within the boundary of the Wheatfield?

30. On the day of battle, what type of fence marked the boundary of the Wheatfield?

31. What reason did Tilton give for withdrawing his brigade in the face of the enemy?

32. Which of Tilton's regiments resisted the order to retreat?

33. What became of Sweitzer's brigade?

34. At what point did de Trobriand order his regiments to retreat across the Wheatfield?

35. After crossing the Wheatfield in retreat, which of de Trobriand's regiments were ordered back to its previous position by Birney, the division commander?

36. Which two regiments advanced over the Wheatfield along with the 17th Maine?

37. Which Federal 2nd Corps division commander ordered his troops to recover the Wheatfield and the northern end of Houck's Ridge?

38. List the brigade commanders of Caldwell's division.

39. List the states that had regiments in Kelly's brigade.

40. Which of Caldwell's brigades occupied the Stony Hill?

41. Which of Caldwell's brigades occupied the northern segment of Houck's Ridge?

42. Which Federal brigade was held in reserve?

Answers:

29. 17th Maine

30. A wooden worm fence

31. Tilton believed his very small brigade of 655 soldiers could not hold the position; also, it was his first battle as a brigade commander. Also, Barnes gave his permission to withdraw the brigade.

32. 118th Pennsylvania

33. It withdrew in good order after Kershaw's regiments' assault on Tilton's brigade.

34. After the withdrawal of Tilton's and Switzer's brigades

35. 17th Maine

36. 5th Michigan and 115th Pennsylvania

37. Brigadier General John C. Caldwell

38. Colonel Edward E. Cross, Colonel Patrick Kelly, Colonel Samuel K. Zook, Colonel John R. Brooke

39. Massachusetts, New York and Pennsylvania

40. Zook's and Kelly's brigades

41. Cross' brigade

42. Brooke's brigade

Gettysburg Campaign Exam Study Guide

QUESTIONS:

43. Edward Cross' Brigade of Caldwell's Division routed which ANV brigade from the southern end of the Wheatfield and out of Rose's Woods on Houck's Ridge?

44. Samuel Zook's Brigade and Patrick Kelly's Brigade of the Caldwell's Division routed regiments of which ANV brigade from the Stony Hill?

45. As Kershaw's regiments were being driven of the Stony Hill, which ANV brigade came forward and through the Rose Farm buildings?

46. From what state did the regiments in Semmes Brigade come?

47. Which AotP brigade replaced Cross' brigade after it ran low on ammunition?

48. Which brigade of the ANV did Brooke's brigade drive out of Rose's Woods?

49. What was unique about the regiments in Day's and Burbank's brigades of Ayers' Division of the 5th Corps, AotP?

50. What two conditions forced Brooke's Brigade from Rose's Woods?

51. Which ANV brigade occupied the Wheatfield Road and assaulted Zook's brigade?

52. Which state supplied the regiments in Wofford's Brigade?

53. List the three Federal brigades that were in reserve at the eastern and northern edges of the Wheatfield while Brooke's, Kelly's, and Zook's brigades were engaged.

54. As the brigades of Zook, Kelly, and Brooke retired from the Wheatfield, which brigades took their place?

55. List the brigades of the ANV that captured the Wheatfield for the final time on July 2.

Answers:

43. G. T. Anderson's Brigade of Hood's Division

44. Joseph Kershaw's Brigade of Lafayette McLaws' division

45. Brigadier General Paul Semmes' Brigade

46. Georgia

47. Colonel John R. Brooke's brigade

48. Paul Semmes brigade

49. The brigades were U.S. Regular Army soldiers.

50. Each soldier had approximately five cartridges left, and remnants of Anderson's and Semmes brigades assaulted Brooke's Brigade

51. Brigadier General William T. Wofford's brigade of McLaws' Division

52. Georgia

53. Sweitzer's Brigade, Burbank's Brigade, and Day's Brigade

54. The brigades of Sweitzer, Burbank and Day

55. From north to south: Wofford, Kershaw, Semmes and Anderson brigades

Gettysburg Campaign Exam Study Guide

QUESTIONS:

56. Colonel Harrison Jeffords of the 4th Michigan saw his colors seized in the Wheatfield, and he died attempting to retrieve them. In what brigade was the 4th Michigan?

Answers:

56. Sweitzer' Brigade

SECTION TWENTY-THREE
Essential Monuments: July 2, National Cemetery, Evergreen Cemetery

High Water Mark Monument, Hancock Avenue (c. 1913). View showing base and bronze book, with granolithic cement plaza, looking west. Copse that firm. Tipton #2340

Gettysburg Campaign Exam Study Guide

July 2, National Cemetery, Evergreen Cemetery

1. Pennsylvania State Memorial, Hancock Avenue
2. 1st Minnesota Volunteer Regiment, Hancock Avenue
3. 13th Vermont Volunteer Infantry, Hancock Avenue

4. Vermont State Monument, Brigadier George Stannard, Hancock Avenue
5. Brigadier General John Gibbon, Hancock Avenue
6. United States Regular Army Monument, Hancock Avenue

7. 42 New York Volunteer Infantry, Hancock Avenue
8. High Water Mark of the Rebellion, Hancock Avenue
9. Major General George Gordon Meade, Hancock Avenue

Gettysburg Campaign Exam Study Guide

1	2	3
4	5	6
7	8	9

July 2, National Cemetery, Evergreen Cemetery

1. Brigadier General Alexander Webb, Hancock Avenue
2. 1st Pennsylvania Cavalry Regiment, Hancock Avenue
3. 72nd Pennsylvania Volunteer Regiment, Hancock Avenue

4. 69th Pennsylvania Volunteer Regiment, Hancock Avenue
5. 111th New York Volunteer Infantry, Hancock Avenue
6. Albert Woolson, Grand Army of the Republic Memorial, Hancock Avenue

7. 108th New York Volunteer Infantry, Hancock Avenue
8. Brigadier General Alexander Hays, Hancock Avenue
9. 90th Pennsylvania Volunteer Infantry, Hancock Avenue

Gettysburg Campaign Exam Study Guide

1	2	3
4	5	6
7	8	9

July 2, National Cemetery, Evergreen Cemetery

1. Maryland State Memorial, Hancock Avenue at Taneytown Road
2. Delaware State Memorial, Hancock Avenue at Taneytown Road
3. Major General John Reynolds, National Cemetery

4. New York State Memorial, National Cemetery
5. National Soldiers Memorial, National Cemetery
6. Figure of Plenty, National Soldiers Memorial, National Cemetery

7. Figure of Peace, National Soldiers Memorial, National Cemetery
8. Figure of War, National Soldiers Memorial, National Cemetery
9. Figure of History, National Soldiers Memorial, National Cemetery

Gettysburg Campaign Exam Study Guide

July 2, National Cemetery, Evergreen Cemetery

1. Figure of The Genius of Liberty, National Soldiers Memorial, National Cemetery
2. Grave site of Virginia Wade [citizen], Evergreen Cemetery
3. 1st Minnesota Volunteer Infantry Memorial Urn, National Cemetery
4. Lincoln Address Memorial, National Cemetery
5. 136th New York Volunteer Infantry, Taneytown Road opposite National Cemetery
6. Brevet Major General Charles Collis Memorial, National Cemetery
7. Kentucky Memorial, National Cemetery
8. Elizabeth Thorn Figure, Women's Memorial, Evergreen Cemetery

SECTION TWENTY-FOUR
The Peach Orchard and Cemetery Ridge

"Peach Orchard Avenue from Emmitsburg Road (1910). Tipton: #3163

Gettysburg Campaign Exam Study Guide

QUESTIONS:

1. At approximately what time did Brigadier General Buford receive permission to refit at Westminster, Maryland and by what time had his troops vacated the area west of the Emmitsburg Road?

2. Which Third Corps regiments of Brigadier General Hobart Ward's brigade were skirmishing west and north of the Sherfy Farm buildings while Buford was withdrawing his cavalry regiments?

3. While Third Corps skirmishers were west of Emmitsburg Road, which Third Corps batteries were posted on the Emmitsburg Road?

4. State the name of the woods west of the Emmittsburg Road in which Federal skirmishers encountered Confederate skirmishers.

5. From which corps, division and brigade were the Confederate skirmishers encountered by the skirmishers of Ward's brigade?

6. List the three regiments which the 1st U S Sharpshooters and the 3rd Maine initially skirmished.

7. List the causes of the withdrawal of the 1st U S Sharpshooters and the 3rd Maine.

8. Immediately before the ANV assault, who were the commanders of the Federal brigades of Birney's division that occupied the Trostle Farm lane, the Klingle farm and the Rogers homestead?

9. When Sickles was wounded, which 3rd Corps division commander became commander of the 3rd Corps?

10. Which Confederate brigade commander split his troops between the planned assault toward the Wheatfield and the Federal line and along the Wheatfield Road?

11. Which regiments did Kershaw send to attack the Federal line along the Wheatfield Road?

12. From Confederate right to left, give the order of the brigades that assaulted the Peach Orchard salient.

The Peach Orchard and Cemetery Ridge

Answers:

1. 10am and 1 pm

2. 1st US Sharpshooters and the 3rd Maine

3. 1st Rhode Island, Battery E [Buckland's] and 1st New Jersey, Battery B [Clark]

4. Pitzer's Woods

5. Hill's Corps, Anderson's Division, Wilcox's Brigade.

6. 8th Alabama, 10th Alabama and 11th Alabama

7. Wilcox's entire brigade entered the fray and the ammunition of the Federals became depleted.

8. Brigadier General Joseph Carr and Colonel William Brewster.

9. Major General David Birney

10. Brigadier General Joseph Kershaw

11. 2nd and 8th South Carolina and the 3rd South Carolina Battalion

12. Barksdale's, Wilcox's, Lang's

Gettysburg Campaign Exam Study Guide

QUESTIONS:

13. After Kershaw's repulse, which Confederate brigade next assaulted the Peach Orchard salient?

14. Generally, which Federal regiments fought along the Wheatfield Road segment of the salient?

15. Which regiment at first occupied the intersection of the Wheatfield Road and the Emmitsburg Road?

16. Which Federal regiment became skirmishers in front of the Wheatfield Road?

17. Which regiments of Graham's brigade occupied the Sherfy Farm buildings?

18. How many Federal batteries occupied the salient along the Wheatfield Road?

19. How many Federal batteries occupied the salient along the Emmitsburg Road to the Trostle Farm lane?

20. Of Barksdale's Brigade, which regiment assaulted the fields southeast and adjacent to the Peach Orchard?

21. Of Barksdale's Brigade, which regiments assaulted the Peach Orchard at the Emmitsburg Road?

22. From what direction did Barksdale's brigade assault the Klingle farm buildings?

23. From what direction did Wilcox's brigade assault the Klingle farm buildings?

24. Which Federal brigade occupied the left of Klingle Farm buildings?

25. Which Federal brigade occupied the right of Klingle Farm buildings?

26. Which federal battery occupied the Klingle Farm buildings?

27. Wilcox's Brigade consisted completely of troops from which Confederate state?

ANSWERS:

13. Barksdale's brigade of McLaw's division.

14. 141st Pennsylvania, 68th Pennsylvania, 7th New Jersey, and 2nd New Hampshire

15. 2nd New Hampshire

16. 3rd Maine

17. 114th Pennsylvania, 57th Pennsylvania, and 105th Pennsylvania

18. Six [from east to west: Bigelow, Phillips, Clark, Hart, Thompson (4 of 6), Ames]

19. Two [Bucklyn, Thompson (2 of 6)]

20. 21st Mississippi

21. 17th, 13th and 18th Mississippi

22. The south

23. The west

24. Brewster's Brigade, Humphrey's Division

25. Brewster's Brigade, Humphrey's Division

26. Seeley's 4th U. S. Battery K

27. Alabama

Gettysburg Campaign Exam Study Guide

QUESTIONS:

28. Lang's Brigade consisted completely of troops from which Confederate state?

29. After Wilcox's and Lang's brigades swept past the Emmittsburg Road, which Confederate Brigade assaulted the Cordori Farm buildings?

30. Wright's Brigade consisted completely of troops from which Confederate state?

31. On the Federal right of the Cordori Farm buildings, two regiments arrived as reinforcements. To what brigade, division and corps did they belong?

32. On the Federal right of the Cordori Farm buildings, two regiments arrived as reinforcements. What were their unit designations?

33. As the Federal troops retreated from the Emmitsburg Road, what stream did they cross?

34. Federal artillery Captain Freeman McGilvery gathered together artillery pieces that played a significant part in halting the assault upon Plum Run. How many artillery pieces were in McGilvery's line at the height of the assaults of Barksdale, Wilcox and Lang's brigades?

35. Two regiments of which Federal infantry brigade halted at Plum Run the advance of Barksdale's Brigade?

36. Willard's Brigade is in which Federal division and corps?

37. The assaults of which two Federal regiments halted the advance at Plum Run of Barksdales's Brigade?

38. The assaults of which two Federal regiments halted the advance at Plum Run of Wilcox's Brigade?

39. To what brigade does the 111th New York belong?

40. To what brigade does the 1st Minnesota belong?

Answers:

28. Florida

29. Brigadier General Ambrose Wright's brigade

30. Georgia

31. Brigadier General William Harrow's brigade, Brigadier General John Gibbon's division, Major General Winfield Hancock's corps

32. 82nd New York, 15th Massachusetts

33. Plum Run

34. 23

35. Colonel George Willard's Brigade

36. Brigadier General Alexander Hays' Division, Major General Winfield Hancock's corps

37. 125th and 126th New York

38. 1st Minnesota and 111th New York

39. Willard's Brigade

40. Brigadier General William Harrow's Brigade

Gettysburg Campaign Exam Study Guide

QUESTIONS:

41. The assault of which Federal regiment halted the assault of Lang's Brigades' assault on Plum Run?

42. To which brigade did the 19th Maine belong?

43. The assault of Wright's brigade on the Federal center crossed which road and which farm buildings?

44. List the regiments in Wright's Brigade.

45. Troops of which two of Wright's regiments possibly crossed the stone wall that ran along The Copse of Trees?

46. Which two Federal regiments turned back the deepest penetration of Wright's brigade?

47. Who commanded the brigades and division of those Federal troops that turned back Wright's assault?

48. Which four Federal regiments at the stone wall turned back a portion of the 3rd Georgia and 48th Georgia?

49. Who commanded the brigades and division of those Federal troops that turned back Wright's assault at the wall?

50. Which Third Corps brigades were rallied and assisted in the pursuit of Wright's brigade from Cemetery Ridge?

51. Which regiments from First Corps' Roy Stone's Bucktail Brigade assisted in the pursuit of Wright's brigade from Cemetery Ridge?

52. Who was in command of Roy Stone's Bucktail Brigade during the pursuit of Wright's brigade from Cemetery Ridge?

53. Which regiment of Webb's Brigade, Gibbon's Division, Second Corps assisted in the pursuit of Wright's brigade from Cemetery Ridge?

Answers:

41. 19th Maine

42. Brigadier General William Harrow's Brigade

43. The Emmitsburg Road and the Cordori Farm buildings

44. 3rd Georgia, 22nd Georgia, 48th Georgia

45. 22nd Georgia and a portion of the 3rd Georgia

46. 13th Vermont and the 20th Massachusetts

47. 13th Vermont: Brigadier General George Stannard's Brigade, Major General Abner Doubleday's Division.
    20th Massachusetts: Colonel Norman Hall's Brigade, Brigadier General John Gibbon, 2nd Corps

48. 7th Michigan, 59th New York, 69th Pennsylvania and the 106th Pennsylvania

49. 7th Michigan and 59th New York: Colonel Norman Hall's brigade
    69th Pennsylvania and 106th Pennsylvania: Brigadier General Alexander Webb's brigade

50. Brewster's and Carr's brigades

51. 149th and 150th Pennsylvania Volunteer Infantry

52. Colonel Edmund Dana

53. 106th Pennsylvania Infantry

Gettysburg Campaign Exam Study Guide

QUESTIONS:

54. Which regiments from a Twelfth Corps brigade recaptured Bigelow's artillery pieces at the Trostle Farm?

55. Which brigade of Hays' Division, Second Corps pursued Wilcox's Brigade and Lang's Brigade, crossed Plum Run, and went beyond its west bank?

56. Which Fifth and Sixth Corps brigades halted the Confederate advance toward the west slopes of Little Round Top and Munshower's Knoll?

57. Which Fifth Corps brigade ascended Little Round Top and took a position on the west slope of Little Round Top, the saddle between the Round Tops and to the crest of Big Round Top?

58. To what position was the 20th Maine moved when Fisher's Brigade took its position?

59. To what unique division did Fisher's and McCandless' Brigade belong, and who was it commander?

60. List the Confederate commanders killed or wounded during the attacks of Longstreet and Hill on the Army of the Potomac's left flank on July 2.

61. During the late afternoon of July 2, to reinforce his left flank Meade removed most of the troops from upper and lower Culp's Hill. Which Twelfth Corps brigade was left on Culp's Hill?

62. During the late afternoon of July 2, to reinforce his left flank, Meade removed most of the troops from upper and lower Culp's Hill. Portions of which two First Corps brigades were left on Culp's Hill?

ANSWERS:

54. Lockwood's Brigade

55. Willard's Brigade

56. McCandless [Fifth Corps] and Nevin [Sixth Corps]

57. Fisher's Brigade

58. The crest of the southwest slope of Big Round Top

59. The Pennsylvania Reserve Division, Brigadier General Samuel Crawford commanding.

60. Hood, Tige Anderson, Barksdale, Pender

61. Brigadier General George S. Greene's Brigade

62. Cutler's Brigade and Meredith's [Iron] Brigade

―― SECTION TWENTY-FIVE ――
Essential Monuments

"Bronze itinerary tablets of Army of the Potomac at East Cemetery Hill on Baltimore Pike (1908)" Tipton #2938

Gettysburg Campaign Exam Study Guide

Essential Monuments

1. 6th New Jersey Volunteer Infantry [DeTrobriand Road]
2. 4th Maine Volunteer Infantry [Crawford Avenue]
3. 16th Michigan Volunteer Infantry [south slope of Little Round Top]

4. Brigadier General Samuel Crawford [Crawford Avenue]
5. 4th New York Independent Artillery {Smith's} [Sickles Avenue at Devils Den]
6. 99th Pennsylvania Volunteer Infantry [Sickles Avenue at Devils Den]

7. 124th New York Volunteer Infantry {Colonel Van Horn Ellis} [Sickles Avenue at Devils Den]
8. 86th New York Volunteer Infantry [Sickles Avenue]
9. 20th Indiana Volunteer Infantry [DeTrobriand Road at Sickles Avenue]

Gettysburg Campaign Exam Study Guide

Essential Monuments

1. 2nd Delaware Volunteer Infantry [Brooke Avenue]
2. 64th New York Volunteer Infantry [Brooke Avenue]
3. 53rd Pennsylvania Volunteer Infantry [Brooke Avenue]

4. 27th Connecticut Volunteer Infantry [Wheatfield Avenue at Ayers Avenue]
5. 145th Pennsylvania Volunteer Infantry [Brooke Avenue]
6. 110th Pennsylvania Volunteer Infantry [Brooke Avenue]

1. 90th Pennsylvania Volunteer Infantry [Hancock Avenue]
2. 115th Pennsylvania Volunteer Infantry [DeTrobriand Road]
3. 17th Maine Volunteer Infantry [DeTrobriand Road]

Gettysburg Campaign Exam Study Guide

1. 62nd Pennsylvania Volunteer Infantry [DeTrobriand Road]
2. 4th Michigan Volunteer Infantry [DeTrobriand Road]
3. 11th Pennsylvania Reserves/ 40th Pennsylvania Volunteer Infantry [Ayers Road at Wheatfield Road]
4. 6th Pennsylvania Reserves/ 35th Pennsylvania Volunteer Infantry [Wheatfield Road]
5. 1st Pennsylvania Reserves/30th Pennsylvania Volunteer Infantry [Ayers Avenue]
6. 2nd Pennsylvania Reserves/ 31st Pennsylvania Volunteer Infantry [Ayers Avenue]
7. 148th Pennsylvania Volunteer Infantry [Ayers Avenue]
8. 27th Connecticut Volunteer Infantry [in the Wheatfield near Ayers Avenue]
9. 61st New York Volunteer Infantry [in the Wheatfield near Ayers Avenue]

Gettysburg Campaign Exam Study Guide

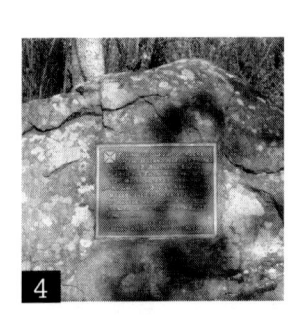

Essential Monuments

1. 1st New York Artillery, Battery D {Winslow's} [in the Wheatfield]
2. 5th New York Volunteer Infantry, Sickles Avenue
3. 17th Maine Volunteer Infantry, [DeTrobriand Road]

4. 32nd Massachusetts Volunteer Infantry field dressing station [Sickles Avenue]
5. 5th Michigan Volunteer Infantry [Sickles Avenue]
6. 66th New York Volunteer Infantry [Sickles Avenue]

7. 52nd New York Volunteer Infantry [Sickles Avenue]
8. 32nd Massachusetts Volunteer Infantry [Sickles Avenue]
9. 1st Massachusetts Sharpshooters, 2nd Company [Sickles Avenue]

Gettysburg Campaign Exam Study Guide

1
2
3
4
5
6
7
8
9

88

Essential Monuments

1. 118th Pennsylvania Volunteer Infantry, [Sickles Avenue]
2. 140th Pennsylvania Volunteer Infantry [Sickles Avenue]
3. 116th Pennsylvania Volunteer Infantry [Sickles Avenue]

4. 98th Pennsylvania Volunteer Infantry [J. Weikert Farmstead on Wheatfield Road]
5. 9th Massachusetts Battery {Bigelow} [Wheatfield Road]
6. 5th Massachusetts Battery {Phillips} [Wheatfield Road]

7. 15th New York Battery {Hart's} [Wheatfield Road]
8. 3rd Michigan Volunteer Infantry [southeast corner of Peach Orchard at Emmitsburg Road]
9. 2nd New Hampshire Volunteer Infantry, [southeast corner of Peach Orchard at Emmitsburg Road]

Gettysburg Campaign Exam Study Guide

Essential Monuments

1. 68th Pennsylvania Volunteer Infantry [Peach Orchard, Emmitsburg Road]

2. Pennsylvania Light Artillery, Battery C {Thompson's} [Peach Orchard at Wheatfield Road]

3. 63rd Pennsylvania Volunteer Infantry [Millerstown Road at Emmitsburg Road]

4. Pennsylvania Light Artillery, Battery F {Hampton's}, [Peach Orchard at Wheatfield Road]

5. 73rd New York Volunteer Infantry {4th Excelsior, 2nd Fire Zouaves} [Sickles Avenue at Emmitsburg Road]

6. 7th New Jersey Volunteer Infantry, [between Wheatfield and United States Avenues and near Sickles Avenue]

7. Excelsior Brigade {70th, 71st, 72nd, 73rd, 74th New York Volunteer Infantry} [Sickles Avenue between Wheatfield and United States Avenue]

8. 120th New York Volunteer Infantry [Sickles Avenue between Wheatfield and United States Avenue]

9. 11th Massachusetts Volunteer Infantry [intersection of Sickles Avenue and Emmitsburg Road]

Gettysburg Campaign Exam Study Guide

1	2	3
4	5	6
7	8	9

Essential Monuments

1. Wisconsin Sharpshooters, Company G, 1st U.S. Sharpshooters, Infantry [intersection of Sickles Avenue and Emmitsburg Road]

2. 1st Massachusetts Volunteer Infantry [north of intersection of Sickles Avenue and Emmitsburg Road]

3. 26th Pennsylvania Volunteer Infantry [north of intersection of Sickles Avenue and Emmitsburg Road]

4. Major General James Longstreet [West Confederate Avenue in Pitzer's Woods]

5. 155th Pennsylvania Volunteer Regiment [north slope of Little Round Top, Sykes Avenue]

6. 121st New York Volunteer Infantry [north slope of Little Round Top, Sykes Avenue]

7. 37th Massachusetts Volunteer Infantry [Sedgwick Avenue]

8. 4th Pennsylvania Volunteer Cavalry [Hancock Avenue]

9. 148th Pennsylvania Volunteer Infantry [Hancock Avenue]

SECTION TWENTY-SIX
EWELL'S ASSAULT ON CULP'S HILL AND EAST CEMETERY HILL: JULY 2 4:00P TO 11:00P

General Richard S. Ewell, Second Corps commander. From a photograph by Cook.

Gettysburg Campaign Exam Study Guide

QUESTIONS:

1. During the late hours of July 2, portions of which AotP First Corps division occupied the crest of Culp's Hill and McKnight's Knoll?
2. During the late hours of July 2, which AotP First Corps brigades occupied the crest of Culp's Hill and McKnight's Knoll?
3. Who commanded the Twelfth Corps brigade that connected to the right of the First Corps brigades?
4. Who commanded the division in which Greene's brigade was located?
5. What significant order did Greene give to his troops that improved their position?
6. Who commanded the Twelfth division that held the position to the right of Greene's brigade?
7. What Twelfth Corps two command structure complications arose on July 1 that continued to complicate the command and control of Federal troops through July 2 and 3?
8. In relation to Rock Creek, where were Federal skirmishers located?
9. Where was Slocum's headquarters located?
10. Upon what topographic feature was Major Joseph Latimer of Johnson's Division, Ewell's Corps, ordered to place artillery and bombard the Federals on Culp's Hill?
11. State the name of the road that bisects Benner's Hill.
12. How many artillery pieces did Latimer place upon Benner's Hill?
13. What factor did the road that bisects Benner's Hill play in the position of Latimer's artillery pieces?

Answers

1. Wadworth's division

2. Meredith's Brigade and Cutler's Brigade

3. Brigadier General George S. Greene

4. Brigadier General John W. Geary

5. Dig and build breastworks

6. Brigadier General Alpheus Williams

7. [1.] Major General Henry Slocum believed he was in command of the right wing of the Army of the Potomac; Slocum turned over the command of the Twelfth Corps to Brigadier General Alpheus Williams; Williams turned over command of his division to Brigadier General Ruger; Ruger turned over his brigade to Colonel Silas Colgrove.

   [2.] Also Brigadier General Henry Lockwood arrived with two regiments and he outranked Ruger by seniority; Slocum designated Lockwood as having an independent command that reported directly to himself [Slocum].

8. Along the west bank

9. Powers' Hill

10. Benner's Hill

11. Hanover Road

12. 22

13. 16 were south of the Hanover Road, and 6 were north of the Hanover Road

Gettysburg Campaign Exam Study Guide

QUESTIONS:

14. At approximately what time did Confederate artillery begin bombardment of the Federals on Culp's Hill?

15. During the Confederate bombardment, how many Federal cannons were on Culp's Hill?

16. During the bombardment how many Federal artillery pieces engaged the Confederate pieces?

17. From what hills did Federal artillery engage Latimer's artillery line?

18. How long did the duel between Confederate and Federal artillery duel last?

19. At approximately what time on July 2 did Slocum order Twelfth Corps troops to move from upper and lower Culp's Hill and toward the Federal right flank?

20. At approximately at what time did Geary receive Slocum's order to withdraw troops from Culp's Hill and move them toward the Federal left flank?

21. Which brigades moved away from lower and upper Culp's Hills and toward the AotP's left?

22. What error did Geary make during the march toward the Federal right flank?

23. From which state was each of the regiments in Greene's brigade recruited?

24. Approximately how many soldiers were in Greene's Brigade?

25. During the Confederate infantry assault, how many Federal cannons were on Culp's Hill?

ANSWERS

14. Approximately 5:00p

15. One

16. Approximately 36

17. McKnight's [Stevens'] Knoll, East Cemetery Hill and Cemetery Hill

18. Approximately 90 minutes, from about 5:30p to approximately 7:00p

19. Approximately 6:00p

20. Approximately 7:00p.

21. Colonel Charles Candy's Brigade and Brigadier General Thomas Kane's Brigade of Brigadier John Geary's Division; Colonel Archibald McDougall's Brigade, Colonel Silas Colgrove's Brigade, and Brigadier General Henry Lockwood's Brigade of Brigadier General Thomas Ruger's Division

22. Marching southeast on the Baltimore Pike, he missed the left turn on to the Granite Schoolhouse Lane. He continued on the Baltimore Pike until he reached Rock Creek. At that point he ordered the troops to countermarch.

23. New York

24. 1,400

25. Five

Gettysburg Campaign Exam Study Guide

QUESTIONS:

26. What terrain obstacles did Major General Edward Johnson face during its assault on Culp's Hill?

27. Johnson's Division contained a brigade commanded by Colonel Jesse Williams. From which state was each of the regiments recruited?

28. Johnson's Division contained a brigade commanded by Brigadier General George Steuart. From which states were these regiments recruited?

29. Johnson's Division contained a brigade commanded by Brigadier General John M. Jones. From which state was each of the regiments recruited?

30. At approximately what time did Johnson's Division enter the woods of the east slope of Culp's Hill?

31. Which of Greene's regiments were skirmishers from before the Confederate artillery barrage and until the beginning of the Confederate assault?

32. Which Federal regiment was alone on the far right of the Federal line that ended on Culp's Hill? State the name of its commander.

33. From north to south, what was the alignment of the brigades of Johnson's division?

34. In Johnson's Division, which two regiments of Steuart's brigade fought through the 'saddle' between upper and lower Culp's Hill?

35. The 3rd North Carolina and the 1st Maryland Battalion were caught in a crossfire between which two Federal regiments?

36. In Johnson's Division, which two regiments of Steuart's brigade fought on the lower Culp's Hill?

37. Which division of Ewell's Corps assaulted East Cemetery Hill?

38. Which two of Early's four brigade's assaulted East Cemetery Hill?

39. Who commanded the brigade that functioned as the reserve brigade for Hays' and Avery's assault?

Answers

26. Johnson had to cross Rock Creek and reform ranks, climb a steep, wooded hillside that kept the gun smoke in the woods, and face an enemy behind breastworks

27. Louisiana

28. Maryland, Virginia, North Carolina

29. Virginia

30. Approximately 7:30p

31. 78th New York

32. 137th New York, Colonel David Ireland

33. Jones, Williams, Steuart brigades

34. 3rd North Carolina, 1st Maryland Battalion

35. 149th New York and the 137th New York

36. 37th Virginia, 23rd Virginia, 10th Virginia

37. Early's Division

38. Brigadier General Harry Hays' brigade and Colonel Issac Avery 's Brigade

39. Brigadier John B. Gordon

Gettysburg Campaign Exam Study Guide

QUESTIONS:

40. Brigadier General Francis Barlow was wounded on July 1. Who took command of his 11th Corps division?

41. Which of the brigades in the Barlow/Ames brigade first met Early's division assault on East Cemetery Hill?

42. On July 1, who commanded Harris' brigade?

43. Which Federal brigade was in support of von Gilsa's and Harris' brigades, but was ordered to the relief of Brigadier General George Greene's Brigade on Culp's Hill?

44. Who commanded Von Amberg's brigade on July 1?

45. When Von Amberg's brigade arrived on Culp's Hill, the brigade was divided. Which two regiments reinforced the left of Greene's line?

46. When Steuart's Confederate brigade captured the abandoned breastworks on the right of the 137th New York, which Federal troops did they encounter west of the breastworks?

47. Brigadier General Harry Hays' brigade was composed entirely of soldiers from which state?

48. Colonel Issac Avery's brigade was composed entirely of soldiers from which state?

49. Of Hays' brigade and Avery's brigade routes to East Cemetery Hill, which one had the longest route?

50. Which main road crosses the crest of East Cemetery Hill?

51. What is the name of the road Harris' ad Von Gilsa's troops defended?

52. During Ewell's assault on Culp's Hill and East Cemetery Hill, which of his divisions was preparing to make an assault on the west slope of Cemetery Hill?

53. Which brigade commander in Rodes' Division was wounded in 1862 at Malvern Hill, which bears a similarity to Cemetery Hill?

54. What was the position of Ramseur's brigade as it related to the other four brigades that were making the assault?

ANSWERS

40. Brigadier General Adelbert Ames

41. Colonel Leopold von Gilsa's brigade and Colonel Andrew Harris's brigade

42. Brigadier General Adelbert Ames

43. Colonel George Von Amsberg's brigade

44. Brigadier General Alexander Schimmelfennig

45. 61st Ohio and 157th New York

46. 61st Ohio and 157th New York

47. Louisiana

48. North Carolina

49. Avery's brigade has the longest route

50. The Baltimore Pike

51. Brick Yard Lane

52. Rodes' Division

53. Brigadier Stephen Ramseur

54. It was the center brigade and designated as the brigade upon which the other brigades would align.

Gettysburg Campaign Exam Study Guide

Questions:

55. When Early's assault got underway, the regiments from which brigade did Hancock send for support to the crest of Cemetery Hill?

56. Hancock also ordered Brigadier General Alexander Webb to send two of his brigade's regiments to the crest of Cemetery Hill. Which two did he select to send?

57. Which two of regiments of Hay's Brigade hit the Federal line first?

58. Which two regiments of Avery's Brigade took heavy artillery fire on their left flank from McKnight's Knoll?

59. What was the name of the Federal officer who was in command of the six pieces on McKnight's Knoll? What was the unit designation of the battery?

60. Which was the last Federal infantry regiment to withdraw from the north end of the Brick Yard Lane?

61. Colonel Wlodzimierz Kryzanowski of the 3rd Division, 11th Corps ordered two of his regiments to north end of the Baltimore Pike west of the Brick Yard Lane. Which regiments were these?

62. List the names of the commanders and their Federal batteries that were nearly overrun by Hay's Brigade.

63. List the names of the commanders and their Federal battery that were nearly overrun by Avery's Brigade.

64. Which eleventh Corps brigade was ordered to assault Hay's Brigade as it crested Cemetery Hill?

65. What was the unit number of the West Virginia regiment that helped save Rickett's battery?

66. What was the unit number of the Indiana regiment that helped save Rickett's battery?

67. Hays mistook Federal troops reinforcing the crest of Cemetery Hill for Confederate troops. Who was the commander of the brigades that Hays' was expecting?

Answers

55. Colonel Samuel Carroll's Brigade

56. 71st and 106th Pennsylvania

57. 7th and 8th Louisiana

58. 21st and 57th North Carolina

59. Lieutenant Edward Whittier, 5th Maine Light Artillery Battery, First Corps

60. 75th Ohio

61. 58th and 119th New York

62. Captain Michael Wiedrich [1st New York, Battery I, Eleventh Corps Artillery Reserve], Captain Bruce Ricketts, 1st Pennsylvania Light Artillery, Batteries F & G, AotP Artillery Reserve

63. Lieutenant George Breck, [1st New York Light, Batteries E & L, Artillery Reserve, First Corps' Artillery Reserve]

64. Colonel Charles Coster's Brigader

65. 7th

66. 14th

67. Major General Robert Rodes

Gettysburg Campaign Exam Study Guide

Questions:

68. What factors caused Hays to mistake Federal troops for Rodes' troops?

69. At what topographical feature did the reserve troops under Gordon halt?

70. Late in the evening of July 2, the 1st North Carolina of Steuart's Brigade fired into the back of which two other of Steuart's regiments who were fighting in the saddle between upper and lower Culp's Hill?

71. Which of Steuart's Brigade achieved flanking the 137th New York out of the breastworks on lower Culp's Hill?

72. Which two battered 11th Corps regiments that came to reinforce the 137th New York were driven back by the 10th Virginia?

73. Which two battered 1st Corps regiments that came to reinforce the 137th New York took a position in the breastworks to the immediate rear and left of the 137th New York and successfully resisted the 10th Virginia?

74. At approximately 10pm, as Hay's and Avery's brigades began withdrawing from the crest of East Cemetery Hill, what division began its forward progress to the west slope of Cemetery Hill?

75. What three factors caused Rodes to halt the forward progress of his division?

76. Overall on July 2, what tactical advantage aided Meade in his successful defense of his Culp's Hill to Big Round Top position?

77. After 10:00p in what position were the 11th Corps defenders of East Cemetery Hill located?

78. After 10:30pm, which division returned to lower Culp's Hill?

79. Which road did Geary's Division use in returning the Culp's Hill?

80. After 10:30pm, which Confederate brigade of Steuart's Division leaves its outpost on Hanover Road and proceeds to Rock Creek's east bank?

81. During the battle, who was the commander of the Stonewall Brigade?

Answers

68. The darkness of night and the smoke of battle

69. Winebrenner Run

70. 3rd North Carolina and the 1st Maryland Battalion

71. 10th Virginia

72. 61st Ohio and 157th New York

73. 6th Wisconsin and 84th New York

74. Rodes' Division

75. Ramseur's and Doles' report of massed artillery facing his brigade, the report that Hay's and Avery's brigades were withdrawing from their assault, and the darkness of the night.

76. Interior lines for reinforcing positions under assault

77. The Brick Yard Lane

78. Geary's Division

79. The Baltimore Pike

80. The Stonewall Brigade

81. Brigadier General James Walker

Gettysburg Campaign Exam Study Guide

QUESTIONS:

82. After midnight, which 12th Corps division returned to Culp's Hill?

83. By midnight which brigade of Johnson's Division occupied the Federal breastworks on lower Culp's Hill?

84. Of Johnson's Division, which brigade occupied the Federal breastworks on lower Culp's Hill?

85. When Walker's Stonewall Brigade crossed to the west side of Rock Creek, the position it took was to the rear of which of Johnson's brigades?

86. To take defensive positions and find their own breastworks, what farm lane did Candy's and Cobham's brigades use?

Answers

82. Brigadier General Thomas Ruger's Division

83. Major General Edward Johnson's division

84. Brigadier General George Steuart's brigade

85. Brigadier General George Steuart's brigade

86. The Spangler Farm Lane which began on the Baltimore Pike and proceeded north east to the saddle between upper and lower Culp's Hill

―― SECTION TWENTY-SEVEN ――
MAPS

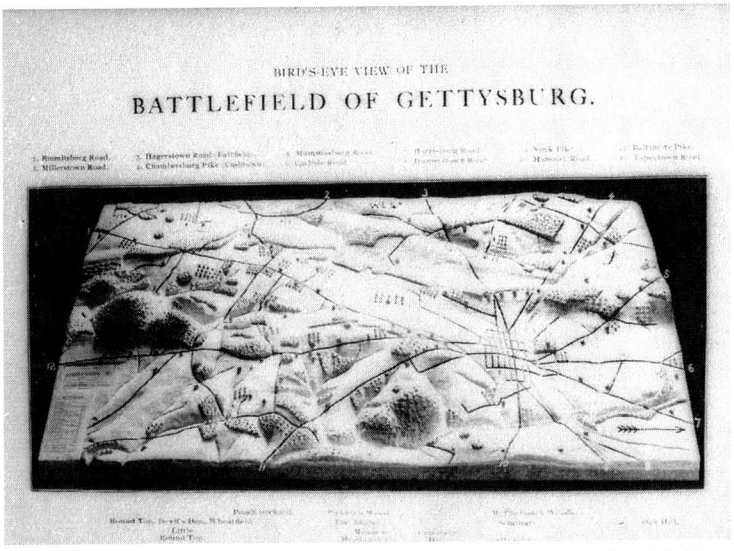

"Copy from book showing Huidekoper's Relief Map of Gettysburg battlefield (c. 1901)." Tipton #3046

Gettysburg Campaign Exam Study Guide

Gettysburg Battlefield
Features in July 1863

0   1 km
0   1 mile

Hills & Streams

1. Herr Ridge
2. Oak Hill
3. Barlow's Knoll
4. Benner's Hill
5. Wolf's Hill
6. Culp's Hill
7. East Cemetery Hill
8. Power's Hill
9. Cemetery Ridge
10. Little Round Top
11. Big Round Top
12. Devil's Den
13. Seminary Ridge
14. McPherson Ridge
15. Oak Ridge
16. Cemetery Hill
17. Munshower's Knoll
18. Warfield Ridge
19. Rock Creek
20. Plum Run
21. Pitzer's Run
22. Willoughby Run
23. Rose Creek

Gettysburg Campaign Exam Study Guide

ROADS

1. Carlisle Road
2. Harrisburg Road
3. Hunterstown Road
4. Gettysburg and Hanover Railroad
5. York Road
6. Hanover Road
7. Baltimore Pike
8. Taneytown Road
9. Emmitsburg Road
10. Fairfield Road
11. Chambersburg Pike
12. Mummasburg Road
13. Newville Road

Gettysburg Campaign Exam Study Guide

FARMS

1. McPherson's Farm
2. Harmon Farm
3. Herbst Farm
4. Forney Farm
5. McClean Farm
6. Hagy Farm
7. Blocher Farm
8. Culp Farm
9. Benner Farm
10. Lady Farm
11. Bushman Farm
12. Slyder Farm
13. Rose Farm
14. Bliss Farm
15. Henry Spangler Farm
16. George Spangler Farm
17. Abraham Trostle Farm
18. Z. Tawney Farm
19. Rummel Farm
20. Cordori Farm
21. Klingle Farm
22. Sherfy Farm
23. Brian Farm
24. Adams County Alms Farm
25. Rogers House

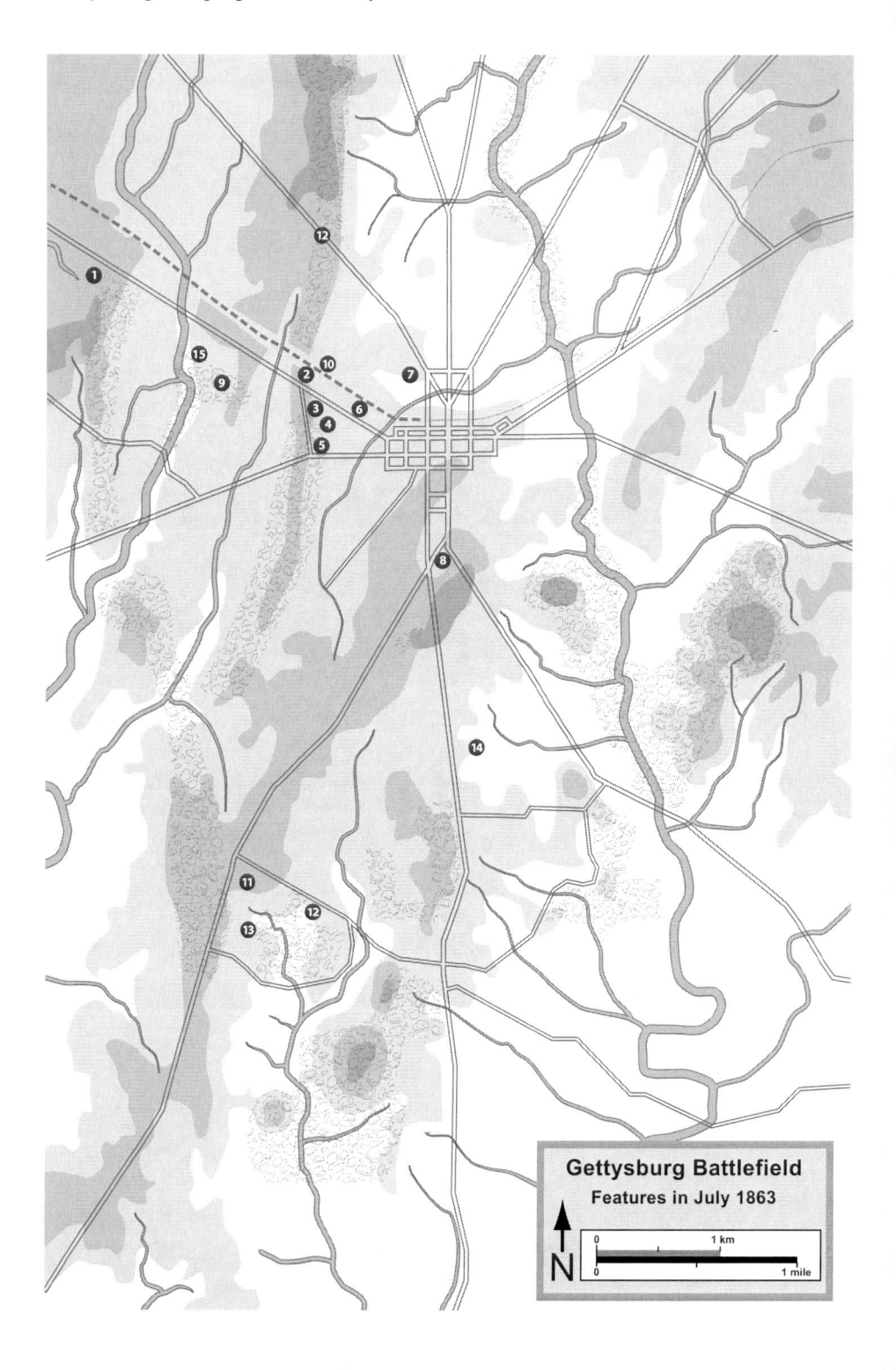

Gettysburg Campaign Exam Study Guide

118

Maps

STRUCTURES, FIELDS, WOODS

1. Herr's Tavern
2. Widow Thompson's House
3. Seminary: Krauth House
4. Seminary: Old Dorm
5. Seminary: Schmucker House
6. Shead's Academy
7. Pennsylvania Hall
8. Wagon Hotel
9. Herbst's Woods
10. Shead's Woods
11. The Peach Orchard
12. The Wheatfield
13. The Triangular Pasture
14. Visitors Center
15. McPherson's stone quarry

―― SECTION TWENTY-EIGHT ――
Essential Monuments: July 2

"DeTroibriand Avenue from near its junction on Sickles Avenue, looking west to Rose Woods and Brooke's Brigade position (1907)." Tipton #3046

Gettysburg Campaign Exam Study Guide

Essential Monuments: July 2

1. Major General Winfield Hancock, Baltimore Road on East Cemetery Hill
2. 4th Ohio Volunteer Infantry, Baltimore Road on East Cemetery Hill
3. 7th West Virginia Volunteer Infantry, Baltimore Road on East Cemetery Hill
4. Major General Oliver Howard, Baltimore Road on East Cemetery Hill
5. 1st Pennsylvania Light Artillery, Batteries F & G [Rickett's Battery], Baltimore Road on East Cemetery Hill
6. 13th New Jersey Volunteer Infantry, Carmen Avenue
7. Indiana Monument at Spangler's Spring at the intersection of East Confederate, Colgrove and Slocum Avenues
8. 1st Maryland Volunteer Infantry [Potomac Home Brigade], Colgrove Avenue
9. 107th New York Volunteer Infantry, Slocum Avenue

Gettysburg Campaign Exam Study Guide

1
2
3
4
5
6
7
8
9

124

Essential Monuments: July 2

1. 46th Pennsylvania Volunteer Infantry, Slocum Avenue
2. 123rd New York Volunteer Infantry, Slocum Avenue
3. 29th Pennsylvania Volunteer Infantry, Slocum Avenue

4. Brigadier General John Geary, Williams Avenue at Slocum Avenue
5. 78th and 102nd New York Volunteer Infantry, Slocum Avenue
6. 1st Maryland Volunteer Infantry [Eastern Shore], Slocum Avenue

7. Brigadier General George Greene, Culp's Hill summit
8. 66th Ohio Volunteer Infantry, Culp's Hill summit
9. Major General Henry Slocum, Slocum Avenue

Gettysburg Campaign Exam Study Guide

Essential Monuments: July 2

1. 147th Pennsylvania Volunteer Infantry, Geary Avenue
2. Pardee Field Monument, Geary Avenue
3. 5th Ohio Volunteer Infantry, Geary Avenue
4. 41st New York Volunteer Infantry, Wainwright Avenue
5. 27th Pennsylvania Volunteer Infantry, Baltimore Road at East Cemetery Hill
6. 17th Connecticut Volunteer Infantry, Wainwright Avenue
7. 25th and 75th Ohio Volunteer Infantry, Wainwright Avenue
8. 134th New York Volunteer Infantry, Baltimore Road at East Cemetery Hill
9. 73rd Pennsylvania Volunteer Infantry, Baltimore Road at East Cemetery Hill

Gettysburg Campaign Exam Study Guide

1

2

Essential Monuments: July 2

1. 153rd Pennsylvania Volunteer Infantry, Wainwright Avenue
2. 14th Indiana Volunteer Infantry, Baltimore Road at East Cemetery Hill

SECTION TWENTY-NINE
July 2 10p to midnight, July 3: 4:30a to 1:00p

Daniel Sickles, Third Corps Commander, and John F. Reynolds, First Corps Commander. Both were dead or wounded by late July 2.

Gettysburg Campaign Exam Study Guide

QUESTIONS:

1. List the names of those commanders and the troops they commanded who attended the late July 2 meeting late in the evening at the Widow Leister's home.

2. State the names of the Federal Corps commanders who were dead or wounded by late in the day of July 2.

3. State the names of the five Federal brigade commanders that had been killed [or mortally wounded] or captured on July 2

4. At this time on July 2, where was Robert E. Lee's headquarters?

5. List the three questions posed by Meade and Butterfield to the commanders in the Widow Leister's home

6. State the names of the two Confederate division commanders who had been wounded on July 2.

7. State the names of the Confederate five brigade commanders who had been killed [mortally wounded] or wounded.

8. Which Confederate corps commanders met with Lee during the late evening of July 2?

9. What orders did Lee issue to his corps commanders during the late evening of July 2?

10. Near about what time on July 2 did J.E.B. Stuart arrive at Lee's headquarters at the Thompson house on Chambersburg Pike?

July 2 10p to midnight, July 3: 4:30a to 1:00p

Answers

1. Meade [commander of the army], Butterfield [chief of staff for the army], Newton [First Corps], Hancock [Second Corps], Gibbon [a Second Corps division commander], Birney [Third Corps], Sykes [Fifth Corps], Slocum [viewed himself as right wing commander but likely seen as Twelfth Corps], Howard [Eleventh Corps], Sedgwick [Sixth Corps],Williams [Twelfth Corps division commander but seen by Slocum as the Twelfth Corps commander]

2. John Reynolds, Daniel Sickles

3. Cross [killed], Graham [captured], Weed [killed], Willard [killed], Vincent [killed] and Zook [killed].

4. Near the Lutheran Seminary and cross the Chambersburg Pike road from Widow Thompson's home

5. [1] Under existing circumstances, is it advisable for the army to remain in the present position or to retire to another position nearer to its base of supplies?

   [2] It being determined to remain in its present position, shall the army attack or wait for an attack by the enemy?

   [3] If the army is to wait for an attack, how long should it wait?

6. Hood and Pender

7. [Tige] Anderson, Avery, Barksdale, Jones, Semmes

8. None

9. Longstreet was to attack Cemetery Ridge; Ewell was to press the Army of the Potomac's right flank; Hill appears to have received no orders during the late evening of July 2.

10. Approximately 2:00p

Gettysburg Campaign Exam Study Guide

QUESTIONS:

11. During the morning of July 3, at what time did Pickett's Division break camp and start its march to the battlefield?

12. During the night of July 2 and 3, how many artillery pieces were situated on Powers' Hill?

13. During the night of July 2 and 3, how many artillery pieces were situated north of the Lightner Farm buildings on the Baltimore Pike and west of lower Culps Hill?

14. Which Federal officer commanded the artillery on Powers' Hill and at Lightner Farm buildings to open fire at daybreak?

15. When did Johnson launch the Confederate assault on upper and lower Culps' Hill?

16. What Federal regiment was ordered to move beyond Greene's breastworks and over the northern crest of Culp's Hill?

17. During the early morning of July 3, how did Johnson arrange his brigades for the assaults on upper and lower Culp's Hill?

18. During the assault on the northeast slope of upper Culps' Hill, which Federal regiment was in the position to fire into the two right flanks of the Confederate brigades?

19. In the middle of the breastworks that ran from upper Culps' Hill to the lower Culps' Hill, there was a traverse which created a 90 degree angle in the breastworks. What significant man-made feature extended southwest from the end of the traverse and was behind the breastworks on lower Culps' Hill?

20. State the name of the commander of the 147th Pennsylvania who moved his troops across a pasture field and towards the stonewall.

21. Besides the 147th Pennsylvania, which other Federal regiments entered the pasture field?

22. During the assault on upper Culps' Hill, what tactic did Greene use when his regiments run low on ammunition?

23. Which of Confederate regiments took a position facing south and at a stonewall facing Spangler's Spring?

Answers

11. Approximately 3:00a

12. 16

13. 12

14. Lieutenant Edward Muhlenberg, nominal commander of 12th Corps artillery

15. When the Federal cannonade ceased

16. 66th Ohio

17. He arranged six brigades in a three brigade front reinforced by three brigades behind them.

18. 66th Ohio

19. A thigh-to-waist-high stonewall

20. Lieutenant Colonel Ario Pardee

21. 1st Maryland [Eastern Shore] and the 5th Ohio

22. As a battlefront regiment withdrew by its right flank, the relief regiment came in on the regiment's left flank.

23. 49th & 52nd Virginia regiments

Gettysburg Campaign Exam Study Guide

QUESTIONS:

24. Which two Federal regiments of Colgrove's Brigade located south of Spangler's Spring assaulted the 49th and 52nd Virginia behind the stonewall?

25. What disadvantage did the 27th Indiana face during the attack?

26. Before 10am Slocum asked Meade for reinforcements to be sent to Culps' Hill. Which units did Meade select?

27. Which two brigades did Sedgwick send forward Culps' Hill?

28. What Confederate regiments assaulted the pasture west of the stonewall and moved toward the traverse and Spangler's Farm lane?

29. Which Federal units contested the Confederate advance through the pasture?

30. At about what time did the Confederate attacks on upper and lower Culps' Hill cease?

31. Brigade by brigade, Johnson pulled his division away from upper and lower Culps' Hill. Where did he place them?

32. As the Confederates retreated, to what location did the Federals advance?

33. Which was likely the last Confederate regiment to fight west of Rock Creek?

34. While the fighting upon Culp's Hill began to recede, what events occurred that prepared for another battle on Emmitsburg Road?

35. Before 10am which Federal officer ordered skirmishers forward to seize the Bliss Farm building from Confederate skirmishers?

36. Which Confederate regiment occupied the Bliss Farm buildings?

July 2 10p to midnight, July 3: 4:30a to 1:00p

Answers

24. 2nd Massachusetts & 27th Indiana

25. It was in the rear of Colgrove's position, and to begin the assault it had to march forward past the 13th New Jersey; the 2nd Massachusetts began its attack before the 27th Indiana reached the location from which it could begin its assault.

26. Meade ordered Sedgwick to send troops to Culp's Hill.

27. Neill's Brigade was sent from Powers' Hill and the Granite Schoolhouse Lane; Shaler's Brigade was sent forward on the Baltimore Pike

28. 3rd North Carolina on the right side of the stonewall, the 1st Maryland Battalion, 23rd Virginia and the 1st North Carolina on the left side of the stonewall, with the 10th Virginia guarding the 1st North Carolina's flank

29. 5th Ohio, 29th & 147th Pennsylvania

30. Approximately 11am

31. Johnson placed his brigades east of Rock Creek.

32. They reentered the breastworks on lower Culp's Hill; from upper and lower Culp's Hill Federal skirmishers were sent forward

33. The 2nd Virginia skirmished with Federal skirmishers coming down lower Culp's Hill and coming north from Spangler's Spring and Creek.

34. The battle for the Bliss Farm buildings raged and Pickett's division approached the battlefield.

35. Brigadier General Alexander Hays

36. 12th Mississippi

Gettysburg Campaign Exam Study Guide

QUESTIONS:

37. Which Federal artillery units were the targets of the sharpshooters of the 12th Mississippi?

38. Troops from which two Federal regiments assaulted the Bliss Farm buildings?

39. Eventually, what drove the 12th Mississippi from the Bliss Farm buildings?

40. Troops of which two Federal regiments occupied the Bliss Farm buildings after the Federal artillery drove the Confederates out?

41. What drove out the 1st Delaware and 12th New Jersey from the Bliss Farm buildings?

42. What was the third regiment that Brigadier General Alexander Hays called upon to assault the Bliss Farm buildings?

43. Which of the Bliss Farm buildings did the 14th Connecticut capture first?

44. How did the Confederates drive out the Connecticut troops?

45. Brigadier General Alexander Hays decided to burn the Bliss Farm buildings. From which regiment did two volunteers take the order to the 14th Connecticut?

46. Why was a Medal of Honor awarded to one of the messengers?

47. How did the Confederates respond to the burning of the buildings?

48. List the brigades in Pickett's division that made the Grand Assault.

49. Which two of Pickett's brigade commanders rode horses forward during the Grand Assault?

50. Portions of which two divisions from Hill's Corps made the Grand Assault?

July 2 10p to midnight, July 3: 4:30a to 1:00p

Answers

37. Cushing's and Arnold's batteries

38. 1st Delaware and 12th New Jersey

39. Artillery fire from Cushing's and Arnold's batteries

40. 1st Delaware and 12th New Jersey

41. Confederate artillery fire from Seminary Ridge and the 12th Mississippi

42. 14th Connecticut

43. The barn but not the house; the house was captured by a second assault by four more companies of the 14th Connecticut.

44. Artillery fire from Seminary Ridge and musket fire from troops in Long Lane

45. 111th New York

46. Instead of crawling to the buildings, a volunteer galloped a horse there and back again.

47. They sent fresh troops and placed artillery fire on the ground around the buildings.

48. Brigadier General James Kemper's Brigade, Brigadier General Robert Richard Garnett's Brigade, Brigadier General Lewis Armistead's Brigade

49. Brigadier General James Kemper, Brigadier General Robert Richard Garnett

50. All four brigades of Pettigrew's Division, two of four brigades from Pender's Division

Gettysburg Campaign Exam Study Guide

QUESTIONS:

51. Who commanded Pettigrew's Division on July 1?

52. List the brigade commanders of Pettigrew's Division that participated in the Grand Assault.

53. List the brigades from Penders's Division that participated in the Grand Assault.

54. Which state enlisted the regiments of Lowrance's and Lanes' brigade?

55. Who led both brigades of Pender's Division into the Grand Assault?

56. How many ANV artillery pieces were committed to the barrage in advance of the Grand Assault?

57. Artillery pieces from which ANV corps were committed to the barrage?

58. List the artillery commanders who were in charge of each corps pieces during the assault.

59. Of the three corps' artillery, which corps' pieces participated the least? Why?

60. How many artillery pieces from Ewell's corps were active during the bombardment?

61. What artillery pieces on Oak Hill contributed to the bombardment?

62. Which officer reorganized and reinforced the Federal artillery line from the George Weikert farmstead to the Evergreen Cemetery Gatehouse?

63. Who was the commander of all the Federal artillery on Cemetery Hill?

64. Longstreet's message that began "If the artillery does not have the effect to drive off the enemy..." arrived to whom and at what time?

65. Longstreet's message that stated, "Colonel, let the batteries open" was given to his corps' artillery commander, Colonel James Walton, at what time?

July 2 10p to midnight, July 3: 4:30a to 1:00p

Answers

51. Major General Henry Heth

52. Colonel James Marshall, Colonel John Brockenbrough, Lieutenant Colonel Birkett Fry, Brigadier General Joseph Davis

53. Colonel Lee Lowrance brigade, Brigade General James Lane

54. North Carolina

55. Major General Issac Trimble

56. more than 160

57. Artillery pieces from all three corps are committed to the barrage.

58. Colonel Edward Alexander [Longstgreet], Colonel Lindsay Walker [Hill], Colonel Thompson Brown [Ewell]

59. Ewell's corps had few adequate topographic artillery platforms to assault Cemetery Hill.

60. 17

61. Two Whitworth field pieces

62. Brigadier General Henry Hunt

63. Major Thomas Osborn

64. Colonel Edward Alexander, approximately 11:15a.

65. Just before 1:00p

141

―― SECTION THIRTY ――
July 3: The Grand Assault

"Bronze work at base of Virginia Monument (background eliminated, showing only the bronze statuary) (c. 1917 or later) Tipton: #2491

Gettysburg Campaign Exam Study Guide

QUESTIONS:

1. Which of Pickett's three brigades suffered the most from the Federal cannonade?

2. What events prevented E. P. Alexander from sending forward artillery support for the Grand Assault?

3. How many Federal artillery pieces were disabled by the Confederate artillery barrage?

4. From north to south, list the order of Pickett's three brigades and Anderson's two brigades during the Grand Assault.

5. From north to south, list the order of Pettigrew's brigades and, in their rear, Trimble's brigades.

6. From what states were Wilcox's and Lang's Brigades?

7. From what state was Marshall's, Lowrance's and Lane's Brigades?

8. From what state was Davis' brigade?

9. From what state was Brockenbrough's brigade?

10. From which states was Fry's brigade?

11. From which wounded general did Trimble take over command of Lane's and Lowrance's Brigades?

12. State the names of the two Federal Second Corps division commanders whose troops bore the brunt of the Grand Assault.

13. State the names of the brigade commanders whose brigades in Gibbon's Division that bore the brunt of the Grand Assault.

14. State the names of the brigade commanders whose brigades in Hays' Division that bore the brunt of the Grand Assault.

15. The Vermont Brigade bore the brunt of the Grand Assault. To which corps and division did the brigade belong?

16. During the artillery barrage, Meade moved from the Leister House on Taneytown Road to what other location?

July 3: The Grand Assault

Answers

1. Kemper's Brigade

2. Alexander's reserve of 8 howitzers and the reserve of artillery ammunition were moved out of Federal artillery range. He did not know to what location the pieces had been moved.

3. 14

4. Armistead's Brigade, Garnett's Brigade, Kemper's Brigade, Lang's Brigade, Wilcox's Brigade

5. Pettigrew's brigades commanded by: Brockenbrough, Davis, Marshall, Fry; Trimble's brigades commanded by: Lane, Lowrance

6. Wilcox's Brigade is from Alabama; Lang's Brigade is from Florida

7. North Carolina

8. Mississippi

9. Virginia

10. Tennessee and Alabama

11. Major General William Pender

12. Brigadier General John Gibbon [Second Division] and Brigadier General Alexander Hays [Third Division]

13. Brigadier General Alexander Webb and Colonel Norman Hall

14. Colonel Samuel Carroll, Colonel Thomas Smyth and Colonel Clinton McDougal [Willard's Brigade]

15. First Corps commanded by Major General John Newton and the third brigade commanded by Major General Abner Doubleday

16. Powers' Hill between the Taneytown Road and the Baltimore Pike.

Gettysburg Campaign Exam Study Guide

QUESTIONS:

17. Which two brigades of Pettigrew's command lagged behind Marshall's brigade during the Grand Assault?

18. Which brigade of Pettigrew's command marched through the smoldering Bliss Farms' buildings?

19. At the beginning of the Grand Assault, between which two farmsteads did the Federal skirmish line run?

20. While Pickett viewed the Grand Assault, between which brigades did he see gaps developing?

21. The Rogers' house, located on the Emmitsburg Road, was on the right flank of which of Pickett's brigades?

22. At what point in Pettigrew's advance did Federal skirmishers begin to withdraw from west of the Emmitsburg Road?

23. Among the Federal skirmishers, which regiments made a brief stand at the Cordori Farm buildings?

24. What impediment did the Bliss Farm buildings offer to Marshall's Brigade?

25. Which Federal regiment in the Emmitsburg Road sent its picket reserve troops out to the west side of the Emmitsburg Road and stymied Brockenbrough's Brigades advance?

26. Which Federal artillery pieces were credited with forcing Kemper's Brigade to move northeast?

27. To which Federal infantry regiment's musket fire did Kemper's left oblique march expose his brigade's right flank?

28. As the Grand Assault crossed the Emmitsburg Road, which two Federal officers ordered artillery reinforcements to the stone wall area?

29. After breaking Brockenbrough's assault, which Federal regiment shifted its left flank 90 degrees and fired into Lane's Brigade?

30. Portions of which two regiments did Alexander Webb order to the wall in support of the portion of the 71st Pennsylvania that remained there?

Answers

17. Davis' and Brockenbrough's brigades

18. Marshall's brigade

19. From northeast of the Bliss Farm to the Abraham Trostle Farm.

20. A gap developed between Kemper and Garnett and another between Garnett and Pettigrew

21. Kemper's Brigade

22. When Marshall's and Fry's Brigades passed through the Bliss Farm buildings.

23. Several companies of the 19th Maine and 106th Pennsylvania

24. Disorganized the ranks and the files

25. 8th Ohio

26. McGilvery's artillery line north of the George Weikert Farm

27. 13th, 14th, and 16th Vermont

28. Brigadier General Alexander Webb and Brigadier General Henry Hunt

29. 8th Ohio

30. 72nd Pennsylvania and 106th Pennsylvania

Gettysburg Campaign Exam Study Guide

QUESTIONS:

31. Who commanded the artillery pieces of the 1st battery of the New York Light Artillery that, as reinforcements, arrived and unlimbered at the Copse of Trees?

32. Which infantry regiment sent volunteers to service Battery A, 4th U.S. Artillery pieces at the stone wall?

33. Which Mississippi regiment moved into the Brien Farm yard?

34. North of the Copse of Trees and at the stone wall that contains The Angle, which two regiments were the last to pull back to the crest of Cemetery Ridge?

35. About 100 soldiers from what Confederate regiment accompanied Brigadier General Armistead when he crossed to the east side of the stonewall which contains The Angle?

36. When Wilcox's and Lang's Brigades moved forward, what resistance did they decisively encounter?

37. When Meade rode from Power's Hill toward the Grand Assault, he discovered both Hancock and Gibbon had been wounded. Whom did he believe was in command of the resistance at the Copse of Trees, The Angle and the Brien Farm?

38. At what location did Lowrance's and Lane's Brigades halt?

39. From which two farmsteads did Pickett view the assault?

40. During its assault, through which farmstead on the east side of Emmitsburg Road did Lang's Brigade pass?

41. After the assault failed at the Copse of Trees, which Vermont Brigade regiment faced to their rear and marched forward to assault Lang's and Wilcox's Brigade?

42. As the 16th Vermont approached Lang's Brigade's left flank, what other regiment did the 16th Vermont find to be firing into the flank of Lang's Brigade?

43. Skirmishers from which regiment occupied Plum Run and slowed Lang's Brigade and Wilcox's Brigade assault on the Federal line?

Answers

31. Captain Andrew Cowan

32. 71st Pennsylvania

33. 11th Mississippi

34. 71st Pennsylvania and 69th Pennsylvania

35. 53rd Virginia

36. McGilvery's artillery line

37. Alexander Hays

38. The Emmitsburg Road

39. The Sherfy Farm and the Cordori Farm buildings.

40. Klingle farmstead

41. 16th Vermont

42. 14th Vermont

43. 16th Vermont

Gettysburg Campaign Exam Study Guide

QUESTIONS:

44. As Pettigrew ordered his troops to fall back from the assault, what happened to him?

45. When Meade approached the Leister House, he ordered the provost guard into the battle. What regiment obeyed his order?

46. What did the 10th New York encounter?

47. To which Confederate commander and regiment did Lee say, "It is all my fault."

48. Which Federal general, while on horseback, dragged Confederate flags in front of the stone wall and Copse of Trees?

49. With Hancock and Gibbon wounded, who assumed command of the 2nd Corps?

50. After the assault failed, Meade ordered reinforcements to the line between Ziegler's Grove and the Copse of Trees. What division did he place there?

Answers

44. His horse was killed and he was shot in the hand.

45. 10th New York

46. Prisoners that needed to be marched to the rear

47. Brigadier General Cadmus Wilcox and the 7th Tennessee

48. Brigadier General Alexander Hays

49. Brigadier General John Caldwell

50. Robinson's Divison, First Corps

— SECTION THIRTY-ONE —

July 3: Cavalry Engagement—East Cavalry Field

"Bronze relief panel on 9th New York Cavalry Monument, Buford Avenue, showing mounted cavalry vidette". Same as #395 (c. 1900) Tipton: #2733

Gettysburg Campaign Exam Study Guide

QUESTIONS:

1. State the name of the commander of the Cavalry Corps of the Army of the Potomac.
2. State the name of the commander of the Second Cavalry Division of the Army of the Potomac.
3. State the name of the brigade commander in Gregg's Division whose troops were posted between Wolf's Hill and the Hanover Road.
4. On July 3 between 10a and 11a Federal Signal Corps troops on Cemetery Hill noticed what development on the Confederate left?
5. How did Brigadier General Gregg learn of this development?
6. Major General Alfred Pleasanton ordered Brigadier General David Gregg to send a brigade to the left flank of the Federal line. Who was the commander of the brigade Pleasanton wanted on the left flank?
7. Who commanded Brigadier General Gregg's second brigade?
8. During the morning of July 3, which crossroads did Custer hold?
9. What topographic feature hid Custer's position from the Confederates' view?
10. When Major General James Stuart was ordered to move his cavalry troops around the Federal right, in what condition were his troops?
11. Who were the commanders of the cavalry troops that were ordered to strengthen Stuart's force?
12. How many artillery pieces and horsemen did Stuart have to move to the Federal right?
13. During the morning, which three regiments did Custer advance as a skirmish line?
14. Though he was ordered to the Federal left flank, how did Custer make the decision to stay at the intersection of the Low Dutch Road and the Hanover Road?
15. How many troops and artillery pieces did Brigadier General Gregg have on the field?

Answers

1. Major General Alfred Pleasanton

2. Brigadier General David Gregg

3. Colonel John Gregg

4. A large body of Confederate cavalry was moving eastward on the York Road.

5. Major General Oliver Howard informed Brigadier General David Gregg

6. Brigadier General George Custer

7. Colonel John McIntosh

8. The junction of Hanover Road and Low Dutch Road

9. Cress Ridge

10. Extremely fatigued and understrength

11. Colonel John Chambliss, Lieutenant Colonel Vincent Witcher, Brigadier General Wade Hampton, Brigadier General Fitzhugh Lee

12. Ten artillery pieces and approximately 4,800 troops

13. 1st, 5th and 6th Michigan

14. Brigadier General Gregg ordered Custer to ignore Pleasanton's order and remain on the field.

15. Approximately 3,400 troops and ten artillery pieces

Gettysburg Campaign Exam Study Guide

QUESTIONS:

16. Which regiments did McIntosh send against the initial thrust of Confederates and what tactic did he order?

17. Which Confederate brigade made the initial thrust toward the Hanover Road?

18. Which brigades did Stuart keep in hidden in reserve?

19. At the center and between the lines are the farm buildings owned by whom?

20. As the firing around the Rummel farm buildings slowed down, what order did Stuart give?

21. Which brigade was the first to charge the Federal center?

22. During the melee between McIntosh's regiments and the second Confederate assault on the Union center, which Confederate brigade commander was wounded by two saber slashes to the head and a bullet wound to the thigh?

23. Which Federal regiment's commander ordered a charge into the left flank of Confederate's second assault?

24. What spectacular tactic did the 3rd Pennsylvania Cavalry regiment accomplish?

Answers

16. 1st New Jersey, 3rd Pennsylvania; the units were to fight dismounted.

17. Lieutenant Colonel Vincent Witcher's brigade and a portion of Colonel John Chambliss' brigade

18. Brigadier General Wade Hampton, Brigadier General Fitzhugh Lee

19. John and Sarah Rummel

20. The brigades of Fitzhugh Lee, Wade Hampton, and John Chambliss were to advance and cross Rummel's fields.

21. Colonel John Chambliss' brigade

22. Brigadier General Wade Hampton

23. 3rd Pennsylvania Cavalry regiment commanded by Captain William Miller

24. The regiment rode through the Confederate charge from east to west, then turned around and rode through the assault from west to east again.

—— SECTION THIRTY-TWO ——
July 2 and 3, After 4p: Pennsylvania Reserves' Counter Assaults

"'The Battle of Gettysburg' painting now in the Pa. State Museum, by Peter F. Rothermel." Tipton: #2669

Gettysburg Campaign Exam Study Guide

QUESTIONS:

1. Who commanded the Pennsylvania Reserves division during the Gettysburg Campaign?

2. To which corps did the Pennsylvania Reserve Division belong?

3. How many brigades of the Pennsylvania Reserves division were at the battle?

4. Who were the brigade commanders during the battle?

5. List the regiments in Fisher's Brigade.

6. List the regiments in McCandless' Brigade.

7. Why did the Pennsylvania Reserve Regiments have alternate Pennsylvania Volunteer Infantry numbers?

8. During the late afternoon of July 2, by what route did the Pennsylvania Reserve Division enter the battleground?

9. To where was Fisher's Brigade dispatched?

10. To where was McCandless' Brigade dispatched?

11. Which regiment did Crawford remove from Fisher's Brigade and place under the command of McCandless?

12. What Sixth Corps brigade was place in reserve behind McCandless' Brigade?

July 2 and 3, After 4p:

Answers

1. Brigadier General Samuel Crawford

2. Fifth

3. Two of the three brigades

4. Colonel Joseph Fisher and Colonel William McCandless

5. 5th, 9th 10th, 11th, and 12th Pennsylvania Reserve infantry regiments

6. 1st, 2nd, 6th, and 13th Pennsylvania Reserve infantry regiments

7. Answering the call for volunteers in April 1861, Pennsylvania met the initial numbers desired and had volunteers left over. They were organized as reserves: 13 infantry regiments, one regiment of cavalry, one battery.

    After the First Battle of Manassas [July 21, 1861] the reserve regiments were ordered into active service and given new numbers. The numbers were their original numbers plus 29. So the 9th Pennsylvania Reserves became the 38th Pennsylvania Volunteer Infantry. The soldiers and commanders preferred their original numbers. The Pennsylvania Reserve division commanders included John Reynolds and George Meade.

8. From Powers' Hill area, marching west, across the Taneytown Road and to the north slope and east slopes of Little Round Top

9. To support Vincent's Brigade in the saddle between Little and Big Round Tops and the west slope and crest of Big Round Top

10. To the saddle between the north slope of Little Round Top and Munshower's Knoll

11. 11th Pennsylvania Reserve [40th Pennsylvania Volunteer Infantry]

12. Colonel David Niven's brigade

161

Gettysburg Campaign Exam Study Guide

QUESTIONS:

13. On July 2 after 7:30p, McCandless' and Niven's brigades charged across which stream and captured what terrain?

14. On July 3 after the Grand Assault, who ordered Major General George Sykes to advance troops as a reconnaissance into Longstreet's positions?

15. Which brigade did Sykes chose for this mission?

16. What did McCandless' Brigade accomplish?

17. How far did McCandless' Brigade move forward after the capture of the 15th Georgia troops?

18. What did McCandless troops observe?

19. In what activity did Fisher's participate?

20. Which two of the Pennsylvania Reserve regiments' monuments are located on the crest of Big Round Top?

21. Which one of the Pennsylvania Reserve regiments' monuments is located near the base of the west slope of Big Round Top?

22. Which one of the Pennsylvania Reserve regiments' monuments is located in the saddle of the west slope between Big and Little Round Top?

23. Where are the monuments of the 1st, 2nd, 5th, 6th, 11th and 13th Pennsylvania Reserves monuments located?

July 2 and 3, After 4p:

Answers

13. Plum Run, and captured a major portion of Houck's Ridge and the J. Weikert farm.

14. Major General George Meade

15. McCandless' Brigade

16. From the stonewall north of Houck's Ridge and west of Plum Ridge, McCandless' Brigade advanced into the Wheatfield, wheeled left, and captured about 100 soldiers of the 15th Georgia and their flag.

17. It moved to the Weikert/Timbers cabin which is west of the Devils Den and the Triangular Field.

18. They reported that Confederate troops were moving from east to west on the Slyder Farm lane.

19. Sharpshooting directed at Anderson's Brigade in Devils Den and defending Big Round Top against Robertson's, Benning's and Sheffield's brigades

20. The 5th [34th] and the 12th [41st] Pennsylvania Reserves regimental monuments are on the crest of Big Round Top.

21. The 10th [39th] Pennsylvania Reserves

22. 9th [38th] Pennsylvania Reserves

23. All are on the west side of Plum Run and on the north end of Houck's Ridge and south side of Wheatfield Road except the 6th's, which is on the north side of Wheatfield Road and the east side of Plum Run.

163

―― SECTION THIRTY-THREE ――
July 3, After 4p: Cavalry Engagements-- South Cavalry Field and Fairfield

"Copied illustration of Cyclorama painting 'Batteries coming into action.'" Tipton: #2771

Gettysburg Campaign Exam Study Guide

QUESTIONS:

1. During the morning of July 3, where were the cavalry brigades of the Federal Cavalry located?

2. When cavalry corps commander Major General Alfred Pleasanton sent Custer's Brigade to Wolf's Hill, which of Brigadier General John Buford's brigades did he send towards Big Round Top?

3. State the name of the division commander who was sent with his troops to the vicinity of Bushman's Hill early on July 3?

4. State the name of the brigade commander who with his troops was ordered to the vicinity of Little Round Top?

5. Who was in command of the Confederate division located in the vicinity of Big Round Top?

6. On July 2 Brigadier General Evander Law took command from which wounded Confederate division commander?

7. On July 3 who commanded the brigade that Laws had commanded on July 2?

8. On the morning of July 3, where on the Confederate right flank were the majority of two Confederate brigades located?

9. By mid-morning on July 3, which regiment of Farnsworth's brigade occupied the far left, near the Emmittsburg Road of the Federal line?

10. Before noon on July 3 which brigade had four regiments of U.S. Regular Cavalry on Emmitsburg Road?

11. From the Emmitsburg Road, which Federal battery began to shell Confederate troops west of Bushman's Hill?

12. Defensive duties on the Confederate right flank were performed by units in Law's Division and which cavalry regiment?

13. What tactic did Merritt's brigade use to drive Confederate skirmishers back?

14. In its front, what topographic feature did Farnsworth's Brigade seize?

Cavalry Engagements-- South Cavalry Field and Fairfield

Answers

1. Around Two Taverns, on the Baltimore Pike

2. Brigadier General Wesley Merritt's brigade

3. Brigadier General Judson Kilpatrick

4. Brigadier General Elon Farnsworth

5. Brigadier General Evander Law

6. Major General John Hood

7. Colonel John Sheffield

8. Eight regiments are located on the west slope Big Round Top.

9. 1st Vermont Cavalry regiment

10. Brigadier General Wesley Merritt's brigade

11. Battery K, 1st U.S. Artillery

12. 1st South Carolina Cavalry commanded by Colonel John Black

13. A dismounted skirmish line along with advancing artillery pieces

14. Bushman's Hill

Gettysburg Campaign Exam Study Guide

QUESTIONS:

15. After what major battlefield event occurred did Kilpatrick order an assault on the lines of the 1st Texas?

16. Describe the terrain to the west of Bushman's Hill.

17. Describe the terrain to the north of Bushman's Hill.

18. What kept Merritt's brigade from pushing further up the Emmitsburg Road?

19. During Farnsworth's Charge, which Federal regiment was first in the assault and broke through the line of the 1st Texas?

20. Who commanded the 2nd Battalion of the 1st Vermont and accompanied Farnsworth?

21. During Farnsworth's Charge, which Federal regiment also assaulted and did not break through the line of the 1st Texas?

22. During Farnsworth's Charge, which Federal regiment in Merritt's Brigade assaulted the far right flank of the Confederate line and pushed it back?

23. Which Confederate regiment successfully defended against the 1st Vermont and then marched across fields, defended against the 5th U.S. Regular Cavalry?

24. Several companies of which Federal regiment were ordered forward in support of the charge of several companies of the 1st Vermont?

25. When 1st Vermont appeared to be trapped, what did Kilpatrick order?

26. Near which farmstead's buildings did combined Confederate troops force the 1st Vermont to divide and then divide again?

27. Three commanders rode in Farnsworth's charge. Describe their fate.

28. What report did Merritt receive which prompted him to send the 6th U.S. Regular Cavalry to Fairfield?

Answers

15. The Grand Assault

16. Flat and mostly free of woods

17. Hilly, rocky with scattered boulders, divided by stone and wood fences

18. The arrival of the 11th and 59th Georgia in front of Merritt's left flank

19. Several companies of the 1st Vermont Cavalry that were led by brigade commander Farnsworth.

20. Major William Wells

21. 1st West Virginia

22. 5th U.S. Regular Cavalry

23. 9th Georgia Volunteer Infantry

24. Nearly all of the rest of the 1st Vermont commanded by Captain Henry Parsons

25. Assault by the 18th Pennsylvania Cavalry and a portion of the 5th New York Cavalry.

26. John Slyder farmstead

27. Farnsworth was killed. Parsons was wounded and escaped. Welles was unwounded and escaped.

28. A farmer from the Fairfield vicinity came to Merritt and reported an unprotected Confederate wagon was located at Fairfield.

QUESTIONS:

29. When the 6th U.S. Regular Cavalry arrived in Fairfield, what did it discover?

30. List the three Confederate regiments that overwhelmed the 6th U.S. Regulars.

31. Who commanded the Confederate cavalry brigade at the Battle of Fairfield?

32. What were the casualties of the Battle of Fairfield?

ANSWERS

29. Very few Confederate wagons moving away from Fairfield, and three Confederate cavalry regiments with an artillery battery coming to Fairfield from the north.

30. 6th, 7th and 11th Virginia Cavalry regiments.

31. Brigadier General William Jones.

32. 6th U.S. Cavalry: 248 killed, wounded and missing; Jones' Brigade: 48 killed, wounded and missing.

SECTION THIRTY-FOUR
FARMS, HOSPITALS AND PRISONERS OF WAR

"George Spangler farm buildings (Eleventh Corps Hospital) from the southeast, with family members standing in field in foreground (c. 1890)". Tipton: #2748

Gettysburg Campaign Exam Study Guide

QUESTIONS:

July 1

1. How many family farms did the battle sweep over and across?

2. At the time of the battle who lived in the Evergreen Cemetery Gatehouse?

3. While his farm was being fought over, where was Edward M. McPherson during the battle?

4. On whose farm is "Reynold's Wood's" located?

5. On whose farm is "The Railroad Cut"?

6. On whose farm are "Iverson's Pits"?

7. Barlow's Knoll was owned by the farmer whose buildings may be seen when facing northwest on the knoll. What is the farmer's name?

8. The Federals' Barlow's Knoll position was flanked on the northeast by Gordon's, Hays' and Avery's brigades. The 17th Connecticut held the farm buildings in the path of this assault. Who owned this farm?

9. The 27th Pennsylvania, 154th New York and the 134th New York held on to the buildings of a brick kiln and other buildings in the brickyard. Who owned this brick manufactory?

10. After noon, North Carolinians assaulting the Federal left on McPherson's Ridge burnt two barns during this advance. One of the barns stood on what would later become the Gettysburg Country Club. Who owned the farm on which the barn stood?

ANSWERS

1. At least 38

2. Elizabeth Thorn, her three sons, her parents. Her husband Peter served as a corporal in Company B of the 138th Pennsylvania Volunteer Infantry; during the campaign he was stationed on Maryland Heights at Harpers Ferry.

3. Living and working in Washington, D.C. as a deputy commission of internal revenue

4. It is located on the 110 acre farm of John Herbst.

5. Edward M. McPherson's farm

6. The farm was owned by John S. Forney who lived there with his wife and infant daughter.

7. David Blocher

8. Josiah Benner

9. John P. Kuhn

10. Emmanuel Harman

Gettysburg Campaign Exam Study Guide

QUESTIONS:

July 2

11. West of the Emmitsburg Road, companies of the U.S. Sharpshooters engaged Alabama regiments under the command of Brigadier General Wilcox. These woods were owned by whom? Who purchased this farm about 90 years later?

12. After the countermarch, Longstreet's troops under McLaws arrived in a position what was bisected by the Millerstown Road. Who owned the farms on either side of the Millerstown Road? Which farmer was also noted for the ridge from which Kershaw's and Semmes' brigades launched their assault?

13. At the intersection of Emmitsburg Road and Millerstown Road, the salient situated at the Peach Orchard was owned by whom?

14. How many bodies of Federals were found in the ashes of Sherfy's barn which the Confederates had burned?

15. Across the Emmitsburg Road from the Sherfy barn was a tenant house. Who lived there and in which army did the tenant's son serve while at Gettysburg?

16. From a farm lane, companies of the U.S. Sharpshooters skirmished against Hood's Division advance. Who owned this farm that was near the west slope of Big Round Top?

17. At the time of the battle, who owned the west slope of Little Round Top?

18. At the time of the battle, who owned the east slope of Little Round Top?

19. State the name of the borough resident who after the war wrote an account of her flight and experiences at the Jacob Weikert farm.

20. At the time of the battle, who owned Devils Den and the slight ridge of which it was a part?

21. At the time of the battle, who owned The Triangular Field?

22. At the time of the battle, who owned The Wheatfield?

Answers

11. Samuel Pitzer, Dwight Eisenhower

12. James Warfield, an African American farmer, owned the land on which Kershaw's and Semmes' brigades was situated; Christian Shefferer own the land on which Barksdale's and Wofford's brigades were situated.

13. Joseph Sherfy

14. 14

15. John Wentz; Henry, his son, was an ordnance sergeant in Taylor's Virginia battery

16. John Slyder

17. Ephraim Hanaway, a stonemason and farmer

18. Jacob Weikert

19. Tillie Pierce

20. John Houck, a borough resident

21. George W. Weikert

22. George Rose

Gettysburg Campaign Exam Study Guide

QUESTIONS:

23. At the time of the battle, on the west side of the Emmitsburg Road, who owned the farm over which Wilcox's brigade assaulted the Federal line on July 2 and July 3? Who lived there?

24. At the time of the battle, on the east side of the Emmitsburg Road, who owned the farm over which Wilcox's brigade assaulted the Federal line on July 2 and July 3?

25. At the time of the battle, on the west side of the Emmitsburg Road, who owned the small farm and whose wife's granddaughter cooked and served food and cared for the wounded in the house?

26. At the time of the battle, who owned and who rented the farm at which the 9th Massachusetts Battery became entangled at the barn and the fence close to it?

27. On July 2, Wright's Brigade crossed the Emmitsburg Road and passed through farm buildings that Kemper's brigade also passed through on July 3. Who owned these farm buildings?

28. East and south of the Hanover Road was a hilltop and farm, which became a Confederate artillery position commanded by Major Joseph Latimer. Who owned this farm?

29. The hill which would become known after the battle as Stevens' Knoll was owned by whom before the battle?

30. On the left flank of the Confederate army, whose farm became a hospital and battlefield during the longest continuous fighting during the battle?

31. Before the battle, who owned and had their name attached to the hilltop that was sold to the Evergreen Cemetery Association?

32. On the east slope of Cemetery Hill, a property owner had both a spring and a pottery shop that include a kiln. What is the name of this property owner?

Answers

23. Henry Spangler; Nicholas and Sarah Eckenrode, with Jacob Eckenrode

24. Daniel Klingle's farm was 15 acres

25. Peter Rogers

26. Peter Trostle owned the farm and rented it to his son Abraham, and Abraham's wife, Catherine.

27. Nicholas Cordori, who rented it to a tenant at the time of the battle

28. Christian Benner owned the 208 acre farm; he lived there with his wife and two sons.

29. James McKnight

30. Henry Culp

31. Peter Raffensberger

32. Edward Menchey

Gettysburg Campaign Exam Study Guide

QUESTIONS:

July 3

33. Who owned the site that would become Major General Meade's headquarters?

34. The spring that is located on the east slope of the lower Culp's Hill and which flows into Rock Creek, is a part of the farm owned by whom?

35. Besides owning the woods in which Colonel Silas Colgrove's brigade fought, for what other activities is James McAllister known?

36. At the time of the battle, who owned Power's Hill, the Federal artillery position and the site that would become Pardee Field?

37. Located between the Confederate lines and the Emmitsburg Road and near Long Lane, who owned the farm buildings that Federal troops destroyed by fire?

38. Who owned the Copse of Trees and most of the farmland between it and the Taneytown Pike?

39. Who owned the small house and barn at the western edge of Ziegler's Grove?

40. The cavalry battle east of the borough and north of the Hanover Road was fought primarily on one farm. Who were the owners?

41. The cavalry battle south of the borough and on both sides of the Emmittsburg Road were fought on farms owned by whom?

42. Of the estimated 51,000 casualties of the battle, how many were prisoners of war?

43. How many prisoners were captured by the Army of Northern Virginia?

44. How many prisoners were captured by the Army of the Potomac?

45. How many wounded and unwounded Confederates were captured by the Army of the Potomac?

ANSWERS

33. Lydia Leister, whose husband died in 1859 and who lived on the ten acre farm with two of her daughters.

34. Abraham Spangler, who lived on his farm located the Chambersburg Pike northwest of the borough, owned a second farm on which his son Henry and his family lived. Spangler's Spring is on the 230-acre farm on which Henry lived.

35. McAllister owned a successful mill on Rock Creek which was also a station on the Underground Railroad.

36. George Spangler

37. William Bliss

38. Peter Frey, whose house was on the Taneytown Pike

39. Abraham Brien, an African American

40. John and Sarah Rummel owned the 123 acre farm

41. The cavalry charge under the command of Brigadier General Elon Farnsworth was on the Michael Bushman farm and the John Slyder farm. The cavalry charge under the command of Brigadier General Wesley Merritt was on the E. Trostle farm and the Heagy farms.

42. Approximate 17,000

43. 5,365

44. 12,227 wounded and unwounded

45. 6,802 wounded and 5,425 unwounded Confederates

Gettysburg Campaign Exam Study Guide

QUESTIONS:

46. Which army commander refused to exchange prisoners on July 4?

47. Which army commander offered prisoners of war a parole?

48. How many accepted this commander's offer for parole?

49. Which division did Lee assign to guard the prisoners of war during their march from Gettysburg to Virginia?

50. Initially, to which two prisoner of war camps did the Confederates assign the Federal prisoners of war?

51. Which Pennsylvania militia regiment was assigned to police the battlefield and gather scattered arms and ammunition?

Answers

46. Major General George Meade

47. Robert E. Lee

48. Approximately 1,500

49. George Pickett's division

50. Officers went to Libby Prisoner and enlisted men to Belle Island; both locations were in Richmond, Virginia.

51. 36th Pennsylvania Militia

Gettysburg Campaign Exam Study Guide

QUESTIONS:

Hospitals and Farms

52. The Catherine Guinn Farm served as a field hospital for which Federal corps?

53. The J. Hummelbaugh Farm served as a field hospital for which Federal corps?

54. The Jacob Weikert Farm served as a field hospital for which Federal corps?

55. The George Spangler Farm served as a field hospital for which Federal corps?

56. The George Bushman Farm served as a field hospital for which Federal corps?

57. The Michael Trostle Farm served as a field hospital for which Federal corps?

58. The Issac Lightner Farm served as a field hospital for which Federal corps?

59. The Nathaniel Lightner Farm served as a field hospital for which Federal corps?

60. The Edwin McPherson Farm served as a field hospital for which Federal corps?

61. The Hugh Culbertson Farm served as a field hospital for which Federal regiment?

62. The Daniel Sheaffer Farm is noted for what particular medical event?

63. The Henry Culp Farm served as a field hospital for which Confederate corps and divisions?

64. The Daniel Lady farm served as a field hospital for which Confederate corps?

65. The Josiah Benner Farm is noted for what particular medical event?

66. The George Spangler Farm is noted for what particular medical event?

184

ANSWERS

52. Second Corps

53. First and Second Corps

54. Third and Fifth Corps

55. Eleventh Corps

56. Twelfth Corps

57. Second, Third, Fifth and Sixth Corps

58. Eleventh Corps

59. Sixth and Twelfth Corps

60. First Corps

61. 6th U.S. Cavalry regiment

62. The amputation of Major General Daniel Sickles leg

63. Second [Ewell's] Corps, Johnson's and Early's Divisions

64. Second [Ewell's] Corps

65. The treatment of Brigadier General Francis Barlow

66. The medical treatment and death of Brigadier General Lewis Armistead

Gettysburg Campaign Exam Study Guide

QUESTIONS:

67. The Samuel Cobean Farm served as a field hospital for which Confederate corps?

68. The Adam Butt Farm and Schoolhouse served as a field hospital for which Confederate brigades?

69. The Francis Bream Farm and Black Horse Tavern served as a field hospital for which Confederate division?

70. Francis Bream's Mill served as a field hospital for which Confederate division?

71. John Socks [Sacks] Mill and Pitzer's Schoolhouse served as a field hospital for which Confederate corps?

72. The Jacob Hummelbaugh farm, located on the west side of Taneytown Road served as a hospital for which Confederate brigadier general who was wounded on July 2 and died on July 3?

73. At which Federal hospital farm house did Tillie Pierce serve as an aide?

74. To which Federal hospital farm were Colonel Patrick O'Rorke, Lieutenant Charles Hazeltt and Brigadier General Stephen Weed taken?

75. At which Confederate hospital farm was Brigadier General Issac Trimble's leg amputated?

76. Bream's Mill Confederate hospital offered medical treatment to which brigadier general who was shot while leading troops in the Grand Assault?

77. Several small AotP Second Corps hospitals were moved a much larger farm which today is site to the Gettysburg Outlet Mall and a hotel. Who owned the farm on which the very large Second Corps hospital was created?

Answers

67. Second [Ewell's] Corps

68. Wilcox's and Wright's brigades

69. McLaw's Division

70. Pickett's Division

71. First [Longstreet's] Corps

72. William Barksdale

73. Jacob Weikert's farm house

74. Jacob Weikert's farm

75. Samuel Cobean farm on the Carlisle [Newville Road]

76. Brigadier General James Kemper

77. Jacob Schwartz

── SECTION THIRTY-FIVE ──
July 4 through 14: Flight and Pursuit

General Robert E. Lee, ANV

Gettysburg Campaign Exam Study Guide

QUESTIONS:

1. At what time and to whom did Lee first issue orders to begin a retreat from the battlefield?
2. At time did the ANV's first wagon train begin to withdraw from the battlefield?
3. How many wounded were in the ANV wagon train?
4. What was the length of the ANV wagon train?
5. At what time did the ANV's second wagon train begin to withdraw from the battlefield?
6. What two roads did the ANV's first and second wagon trains use to depart the battlefield?
7. Who commanded the ANV cavalry brigades that guarded the Cashtown flank of the ANV?
8. Who commanded the ANV cavalry brigades that guarded the Emmitsburg flank of the ANV?
9. Who commanded the AotP cavalry division that was dispatched to Williamsport, Maryland?
10. Who commanded the AotP cavalry division that was dispatched to Emmitsburg?
11. On July 4, what is likely known as the first interception of an ANV wagon train by AotP cavalry?
12. During July 4, what activity did the infantry of the ANV and AoP take?
13. When the ANV infantry began to withdraw from the battlefield what city was their immediate destination?
14. Of the three ANV corps, which one was the last to withdraw from the battlefield?
15. What added responsibility did the ANV First Corps have during the retreat?

July 4 through 14: Flight and Pursuit

Answers

1. Approximately 1a on July 4 to Brigadier John Imboden, who was to provide the cavalry escort for the wagon train
2. Approximately 4a
3. Approximately 12,000
4. Approximately 17 miles
5. Approximately 4a
6. The Cashtown-Greenwood Road and the Fairfield Road
7. Brigadier Generals Beverly Roberstsons and William 'Grumble' Jones
8. Brigadier Generals Albert Jenkins and John Chambliss
9. Brigadier General John Buford
10. Brigadier General Judson Kilpatrick
11. The Battle of Monterrey Pass, Kilpatrick's division and the ANV Second Corps wagon train.
12. They stayed on the battlefield, burying the dead and suffering the effects of violent rain and thunderstorms
13. Hagerstown, Maryland
14. The Second [Ewell's] Corps
15. Escorting 4,000 Federal prisoners of war

Gettysburg Campaign Exam Study Guide

QUESTIONS:

16. On July 5 what unique attack occurred upon the ANV's wagon train as it passed through Greencastle?

17. When did the first ANV wagon train reach Williamsport, Maryland?

18. When did Buford's cavalry division reach Frederick, Maryland?

19. Which corps of the ANV led the movement westward from the battlefield?

20. Which and when did the last ANV corps begin to leave the battlefield?

21. When and which corps did Major General Meade send forward toward the ANV position on July 5?

22. Which ANV Second Corps division and brigade did the Federals first engage in fighting on July 5 at Fairfield?

23. Which two corps of the AotP moved forward and toward Two Taverns and Littlestown the same day but later than the Sixth Corps?

24. When did the AotP's Eleventh Corps join the pursuit of the ANV?

25. Which two AotP corps remained on the battlefield on July 6?

26. Which AotP corps remained on the battlefield on July 6?

27. Which AoP corps did not march on July 6?

28. On July 7, in the vicinity of what location was the ANV encamped?

29. On July 6 and 7, by what means did Imboden send the ANV across the Potomac River?

30. When and which AotP army corps was the last to leave the battlefield?

31. After leaving the battlefield, at what location did Meade make his headquarters?

32. On July 7 and 8, to what location did Federal troops from the Department of the Susquehanna move?

33. On July 7 and 8, to what location did Federal troops from the Department of West Virginia move?

July 4 through 14: Flight and Pursuit

Answers

16. Approximately 35 Pennsylvania civilians attacked the wagon train with axes and chopped wheel spokes of about ten wagons

17. July 5

18. July 5

19. Third [Hill's] Corps

20. Second [Ewell's] Corps, July 5, 2am.

21. Sixth Corps, 8am

22. Early's division, Gordon's brigade at about 5p

23. Second Corps and Twelvth Corps

24. July 6

25. First and Third Corps

26. Third Corps

27. Second, Third and Twelve

28. Hagerstown, Maryland

29. Ferrying by boats

30. July 7, Third Corps

31. Frederick, Maryland

32. South of Greencastle, Pennsylvania

33. The vicinity of Hancock, Maryland

193

Gettysburg Campaign Exam Study Guide

QUESTIONS:

34. On July 8 at what location did Meade make his headquarters?

35. On July 9 at what location did Meade make his headquarters?

36. Between July 9 and 11, between which two Maryland towns did the Federal lines extend?

37. Between July 9 and 14, what was the north to south alignment of the ANV? corps?

38. What was the location of the July 10 fight between the ANV cavalry under Stuart and the AotP cavalry division under Buford?

39. Between July 9 and 12, what was the main mission of the ANV cavalry of Stuart?

40. At what time and day did Longstreet receive orders to begin his corps crossing the Potomac River on a pontoon bridge?

41. At what location did Longstreet's corps cross the Potomac River?

42. On what day and time did Longstreet's corps finish crossing the Potomac River?

43. At what location, day and time did Hill's corps cross the Potomac River?

44. At what location, day, time and means did Ewell's corps cross the Potomac River?

45. At what location, day and time did Stuart's cavalry divisions cross the Potomac River?

46. When and how did Major General Meade learn of the ANV's evacuation of its entrenchments?

47. At what location and from corps were the most ANV prisoners captured by Federal cavalry?

48. Which ANV brigadier general was slain by AotP cavalry on July 14 on the bank opposite Falling Waters, Virginia?

July 4 through 14: Flight and Pursuit

Answers

34. Middletown, Maryland

35. Turner's Gap in South Mountain, Maryland

36. Hagerstown and Sharpsburg

37. Second, Third, First

38. Funkstown, Maryland

39. Screen the ANV's construction of entrenchments from Federal reconnaissance

40. July 13, approximately 5p

41. From the bank opposite Falling Waters, Virginia

42. July 14, approximately 9a

43. From the northern bank opposite Falling Waters, Virginia, July 14, between approximately 9a and 12 noon

44. Williamsport July 13, from late evening through 8a July 14, using a pontoon bridge and by wading the chest high river

45. July 14 from approximately 8a to noon.

46. July 14, approximate 8a, from Brigadier General John Buford

47. From the bank opposite Falling Waters, Virginia; Third Corps

48. Brigadier General James Pettigrew

Gettysburg Campaign Exam Study Guide

QUESTIONS:

49. How many ANV soldiers were captured on the morning of July 14 by AotP cavalry?

50. Besides captured Federal soldiers, what other prisoners did the ANV take across the Potomac River?

51. Besides an attack made by Pennsylvania citizens upon the ANV wagon train at Greencastle what other effort did citizens make there?

52. What caused the AotP's infantry to refrain from attacking the ANV on July 12 and 13?

Answers

49. Approximate 700

50. African Americans to be enslaved or re-enslaved and Adams County abolitionists

51. Between 30 and 40 African Americans were re-captured from the ANV by abolitionists.

52. The extensive fortifications built by the ANV and the flooded condition of the terrain over which the AotP would have to attack

SECTION THIRTY-SIX
The Eisenhower Farm, The George Spangler Farm, The Lutheran Seminary, Gettysburg College, Gettysburg Borough & Letterman Field Hospital

"East elevation of Huber Hall, Gettysburg College (1920s)." Tipton: #4167

Gettysburg Campaign Exam Study Guide

QUESTIONS:

The Eisenhower Farm

1. During what year did the Eisenhowers buy an Adams County farm?
2. How old was the oldest building on the farm?
3. From whom did the Eisenhowers buy the farm?
4. In what year was the construction of a new house completed
5. How many acres did the Eisenhowers own?
6. How many acres adjacent to his personal holding did the Eisenhowers and their business partners own?
7. What breed of cattle did the Eisenhower and their partners raise and exhibit?
8. In what state was Dwight David Eisenhower born?
9. In what state was Dwight David Eisenhower raised?
10. What three hobbies did Eisenhower enjoy while living on the Adams County farm?
11. The herdsman's house on the farm is historic. In what year was it first built?
12. After his graduation from West Point Military Academy, what service did Eisenhower perform during World War One?
13. Between his retirement from the military and his elections to the presidency of the United States, what job did Eisenhower accept?
14. During what years was Eisenhower president of the United States?
15. During what year did the Eisenhowers donate the farm to the federal government?
16. During what year did Eisenhower die, and during what year did his wife die?

Answers

1. 1950
2. About 200 years old
3. Allen Redding
4. 1955
5. 189
6. 306
7. Black Angus
8. Texas
9. Kansas
10. Golf, oil painting and target shooting
11. 1797
12. He was stationed at Camp Colt which was located with the Gettysburg National Military Park and trained soldiers for the army tank corps.
13. The presidency of Columbia University, located in New York City
14. He was elected in 1952 and inaugurated in 1953. He left the presidency in January of 1961.
15. 1967
16. 1969, 1979

Gettysburg Campaign Exam Study Guide

QUESTIONS:

The George Spangler Farm

1. In what year did George Spangler buy the farm?
2. List the buildings that were on the farm at the time of the battle.
3. What was the size of the Spangler family?
4. Which Federal Corps used the farm as a field hospital?
5. How many wounded were received by this field hospital?
6. Currently, who owns the farm?
7. In 1863, which roads bordered or passed through the farm?

8. At the time of the battle, how many acres were in the farm?
9. Among the wounded, how many were Confederates?
10. During the battle what portion of the Union Army was stationed on the farm?
11. During the battle, besides the medical corps and the reserve artillery, what other branch occupied a portion of the farm?
12. How many Union soldiers were buried on the farm?
13. About a century later, which of the buried Union soldiers had a great-grandson living in the White House?
14. How many Confederates were buried on the farm?
15. Which Confederate brigadier general died on the farm? When did he die?

Answers

1. 1848
2. Pennsylvania bank barn, two story stone house, summer kitchen, smoke house, corn crib, latrine
3. Father and mother, two daughters and two sons
4. Eleventh
5. Appromimately 1,900
6. Gettysburg Foundation
7. To the west: Taneytown Road; to the east: Baltimore Pike; to the north: Granite Schoolhouse Road passed through the acres George Spangler owned
8. 166
9. Approximately 100
10. The reserve artillery
11. The Signal Corps occupied Powers Hill in the northern part of the farm.
12. 185
13. George Nixon of the 73rd Ohio regiment
14. About 20
15. Lewis Armistead, July 6

QUESTIONS:

The Lutheran Seminary

1. When was the Lutheran Seminary founded?
2. When did the seminary move to its present location?
3. What position on slavery did the seminary's president take?
4. State the names of the seminary buildings which stood at the time of the battle.
5. Who used the dormitory's cupola during the battle?
6. Who used the dormitory as a hospital during the battle?
7. What misfortune occurred to the hospital during the late afternoon and evening of July 1?
8. To which Confederate hospital were the Federal hospital supplies taken?
9. When did Federal forces recapture the seminary hospital?
10. State the name of the military unit which some students of the seminary joined in June 1863.

Answers

1. 1826
2. 1832
3. He was an abolitionist and provided a way station on the Underground Railroad
4. Old Dorm, the Krauth residence and the Smucker residence
5. The Federal Signal Corps
6. The Federal First Corps
7. It was captured by Confederate forces and looted of all its medical supplies
8. The Confederate hospital at Black Horse Tavern
9. The morning of July 5
10. 26th Emergency Militia, Company A

Gettysburg Campaign Exam Study Guide

QUESTIONS:

Gettysburg College

1. In what year was the current Gettysburg College founded?

2. What was the name of Gettysburg College during 1863?

3. Which academic building is named for a Pennsylvania abolitionist?

4. State the name of the military unit which some students of the college joined in June 1863.

5. On July 1, which Federal corps' troops crossed the college's grounds while they were going into the fight?

6. Which college building became both a Federal Signal Corps observation post and a Confederate hospital during the battle?

7. What additional function did the campus and its two buildings fulfill after the battle?

8. What function did the college's president's home serve during the battle?

9. What position in the National Cemetery dedication procession did Pennsylvania college students take?

10. From which position did the college students listen to Everett's and Lincoln's speeches?

Answers

1. 1832

2. Pennsylvania College

3. Stevens Hall

4. 26th Emergency Militia, Company A

5. The 11th Corps

6. Pennsylvania Hall

7. Continued as a Confederate hospital and also became a location for captured Confederates to be collected

8. A hospital for wounded Federals

9. They were placed at the tail end of the procession

10. They were within a few feet of the front of the speaker's stage.

Gettysburg Campaign Exam Study Guide

QUESTIONS:

Gettysburg Borough and Camp Letterman

1. In what year was the borough of Gettysburg's streets laid out?

2. In what year did Gettysburg become the seat of Adams County?

3. In what year did railroad service arrive in Gettysburg?

4. Of the several photographic studios in Gettysburg during the time of the battle, which one is most frequently related to post-battle photography?

5. With whom did Abraham Lincoln obtain overnight accommodations during his November 1863 visit?

6. Along which east-west street did Confederate battle lines run?

7. State the name of the hotel located at the fork of the Emmitsburg Road and the Baltimore Pike which served as an outpost for Federals who were skirmishing with Confederates.

8. Which building in the borough was used as an observation post by Major General Oliver Howard?

9. On the steps of which church building in the borough was a Federal chaplain killed by a Confederate coming into the town on July 1?

10. State the name of the building on the southwest corner of The Square that housed the United States Christian Commission's offices and stores after the battle.

11. When was Camp Letterman established?

12. When was Camp Letterman closed?

13. How many Union and Confederate soldiers did Camp Letterman have as patients?

14. Which road was Camp Letterman located upon?

Answers

1. 1786
2. 1800
3. 1858
4. The Tyson brothers' studio
5. David Wills
6. Middle Street
7. Wagon Hotel
8. The Fahnestock House on Baltimore Street
9. The Lutheran church on Chambersburg Street.
10. Stoever-Schick Building
11. July 5, 1863
12. November 20, 1863
13. 14,193 Union and 6,802 Confederate which totals 20,995
14. The York Road

QUESTIONS:

15. What characteristics did Letterman look for when choosing a location for a hospital?

16. Which farm and ANV hospital was located adjacent to and on the southern side of Lettermen hospital?

Answers

15. 1. Contained a good spring,
     2. Close proximity of a railroad,
     3. On a major road,
     4. On a cleared elevation that would catch sunshine and a breeze

16. The Daniel Lady Farm

—— SECTION THIRTY-SEVEN ——
100 More of the 175 Things Licensed Battlefield Guides Know

"Unidentified male group standing at west entrance to Wills House, Lincoln Square, Gettysburg (c. 1920s)." Tipton: #4959

Gettysburg Campaign Exam Study Guide

QUESTIONS:

1. What is the Captain David Acheson rock?

2. Where are there James Rifles artillery on the battlefield?

3. Where is location of the monument that marks the wounding of Daniel Sickles?

4. Where is the artillery piece named 'Cora' on the battlefield?

5. What is the significance of the Christ Lutheran Church at 44 Chambersburg Street?

6. Where was the Gettysburg Female Academy located?

Answers

1. The rock is located west of the John Weikert Farm buildings which are located on Wheatfield Road. Captain of Company C, 140th Pennsylvania Volunteer Infantry, David Acheson was wounded while fighting on the Stony Knoll's Loop, then killed while being helped through the Wheatfield. His body was retrieved by comrades immediately after the battle. 'D.A.' was carved into the rock beside his grave. He was disinterred during mid-July and '140 PV' was added to the rock.

2. James Rifles are marking the artillery position of the 2nd Connecticut Battery on Hancock Avenue. They are bronze, and the rifling was put in the barrels during the casting process, not bored into the rifle afterward.

3. The monument is about 20 to 30 yards from the northwest corner of the Abraham Trostle barn which is located on United States Avenue. The location of the marker was likely chose by Daniel Sickles after the war.

4. 'Cora' is painted on the barrel of an artillery piece located on United States Avenue and close to the south wall of the Trostle barn. It is likely that the piece had 'Cora' painted just below the cascabel, at the opposite end from the muzzle, during the war.

5. Before the war the church was called College Lutheran Church. The church building served as a field hospital of the Federal First Corps. Approximately 140 soldiers were laid in the sanctuary by midday. Beds were improvised by laying boards on top of the pews. Horatio Howell, chaplain of the 90th Pennsylvania, was killed on the steps of the church. During the late afternoon of July 1, he was shot by Confederates pursuing Federals though the borough. There is a wayside marker that notes Howell's death.

6. The building at 66-68 West High Street is the location of the Gettysburg Female Academy. Prior to the founding of the academy, the Lutheran Seminary was first organized and held classes in the building. After the seminary moved, Pennsylvania [Gettysburg] College was organized and conducted its first classes in the building. Today, the building has battle damage from artillery visible from West High Street.

QUESTIONS:

7. What is the location and significance of the the Fahnestock Building?

8. Where is the marker for John Page Nicholson and what is its significance?

9. Where is the Sickles Plaque and what is its significance?

10. State the names of the three African-Americans who had residences within the Gettysburg National Military Park at the time of the battle.

11. Who is Private George Washington Sandoe and where is he buried?

12. What is unique about the 21st Pennsylvania Cavalry monuments?

13. How many burials did Virginia Wade have? Where are the burial sites located?

Things Licensed Battlefield Guides Know

Answers

7. Its location is at the intersection of Baltimore Street and Middle Street. On July 1 Major General Oliver Howard used its roof at an observation post.

8. The marker is located on the east side of Hancock Avenue near Ziegler's Grove. Nicholson was a Lieutenant Colonel in the 28th Pennsylvania Volunteer Infantry and a Battle of Gettysburg veteran. He was active in veteran's affairs and a leading member of the commission which created and defined the Gettysburg National Military park

9. The Gettysburg National Military Park Legislation Plaque is also called the Sickles Plaque. It is located near the old Cyclorama's location and on the road that connects the Emmitsburg Road and the Taneytown Pike.

10. Abraham Brian, Alfred Palm, and James Warfield

11. Private George Washington Sandoe became known as the first Union soldier killed at Gettysburg. He was killed on June 26th by Confederate cavalry attached to Early's Division. Sandoe is buried in the cemetery of Mount Joy Lutheran Church which is located on the Taneytown Road.

12. Private George Sandoe, of Company B, 21st Pennsylvania Cavalry. Both monuments are on Baltimore Pike, and both commemorate Sandoe. The monuments are within 100 feet of each other.

13. She was killed on July 3 and buried in the garden behind the McClellan house in which she died. She was buried on July 4 and remained here until January, 1864. Her body moved to the German Reformed Church Cemetery which is located at the intersection of High Street and South Stratton Street. Currently the church building is the Trinity United Church of Christ. The cemetery now longer exists. The third burial occurred in Evergreen Cemetery during November, 1865.

Gettysburg Campaign Exam Study Guide

QUESTIONS:

14. State the name of a general who is buried and has a significant monument in the National Cemetery but was not at the Battle of Gettysburg.

15. State the names of the two Gettysburg College buildings that existed during the battle. Which had a signal stationed in its cupola? Which became a field hospital?

16. In which Gettysburg College building did President Dwight Eisenhower have an office?

17. Which buildings in the borough were built to commemorate the 25th and 50th anniversaries of the battle?

18. List the three houses associated with Virginia Wade.

19. What unit policed the battlefield and what was recovered from the battlefield after the Confederate retreat?

20. What is and where is 'The Fuller Marker'?

Answers

14. Charles Collis did not fight at Gettysburg, but he is the highest ranking individual buried in the cemetery. Collis had been a Colonel of the 114th Pennsylvania Infantry who had been brevetted to the ranks of Brigadier General and Major General. He was never given a permanent rank of Brigadier General.

15. President's House of 1860 and Pennsylvania Hall, which then and now has a cupola and which became a field hospital

16. Gettysburg College office of President Dwight D. Eisenhower is located on the west side of Carlisle Street near its intersection with East Stevens Street.

17. The Prince of Peace Episcopal Church at the intersections of Baltimore and High Streets was built to commemorate the 25th anniversary of the battle. The building which is today the Adams County Library was constructed in 1913 as a U.S. Post Office for the 50th anniversary of the building.

18. Virginia Wade's birthplace is on the east side of Baltimore Street at the intersection of Wade Street. The house in which she lived before the battle is located at 49 Breckinridge Street. The McClellan House is the home in which she died; it is located on the Baltimore Street.

19. The 36th Pennsylvania Volunteer Militia Regiment was sent to Gettysburg, and its commanding officer, Colonel H. C. Alleman, was made Military Governor of the district, embracing the battle-ground. It was engaged in gathering in the wounded and stragglers from both armies, in collecting the debris of the field, and in sending away the wounded as fast as their condition would permit.

20. The Henry V. Fuller marker, is located in Rose's Woods along Rose's Run. And a bit east of the old trolley path. Fuller was commander of Company F 64th New York Infantry Regiment. He was killed on July 2, 1863 as Brooke's Brigade, was retreating through Rose's Woods towards the Wheatfield. His marker was dedicated by the surviving members of his company.

Gettysburg Campaign Exam Study Guide

QUESTIONS:

21. What is the significance and where is the 'Irsch Advance Marker'?

22. Where is Jones Artillery Avenue and what is its significance?

23. Where is the 'First Shot Marker'?

24. Where is the Hazlett Inscription?

25. Where is Menchey's Spring?

26. Where is Trough Rock?

27. Where is the John Forney farm located and what is its significance?

28. Where is the Henry Culp farmstead located and what is its significance?

Answers

21. The marker of the 45th New York is located beside the McLean farm lane north of the Mummasburg Road and shows the regiment's advanced position on July 1st. Captain Francis Irsch was awarded the Medal of Honor for gallantry in flanking the enemy, capturing a number of prisoners, and taking a defensive stance in the town.

22. The avenue is less than a mile northeast of Gettysburg and along Business Route 15. It is a narrow, paved lane with a small strip of park land on either side of it, and obscured by residences and a retirement facility. It ends at a cul-de-sac and located there are the headquarters marker and the four battery markers for Jones' Artillery Battalion of Early's Division.

23. It is located 3 miles west of Gettysburg on Route 30 at its intersection with Knoxlyn Road, The monument is on the north side of U.S. 30 next to a small residence owned by the GNMP.

24. On the crest of Little Round Top near the smaller of the two monuments to the 91st Pennsylvania Infantry Regiment. It reads "Hazlett fell com'r Batt'y D 5 U.S.Art'y in battle July 2nd 1863"

25. It is at the bottom of the east slope of East Cemetery Hill and the west slope of Steven's Knoll. It is on the east side of Wainwright Avenue.

26. It is located in the near Devil's Den and Plum Run. It is a man-made depression in a boulder which at times brings water from the bank behind it. The trough is as high off the ground as a horse's head.

27. The farm is located immediately adjacent to the Eternal Light Peace Memorial and on the south side of the Mummasburg Road. On July 1 Iverson's Brigade passed through the farm buildings to assault the Federals on Oak Ridge. Iverson's Pits are located on this farm. The buildings were removed for the 1938 unveiling of the Eternal Light Peace Memorial.

28. The Henry Culp Farm is located at 301 East Middle Street and northeast of Culp's Hill. It was within Confederate lines and became a field hospital.

Gettysburg Campaign Exam Study Guide

QUESTIONS:

29. Where is the Daniel Sheaffer farmstead located and what is its significance?

30. Where is the George House located and what is its significance?

31. Where is Warfield Ridge and what is its significance?

32. Where is the James Warfield House And Farm and what is its significance?

33. What is the location of Brigadier General Henry Hunt's headquarters marker?

34. Where is the 'Tipton Inscription' and 'Tipton Station' located?

35. Where was John Burn's house located?

36. Where is George Nixon's grave located?

37. Where is and what is the significance of 'Bigelow's Gate'?

Answers

29. The Daniel Sheaffer Farm is located on the Baltimore Pike, a bit southeast of Route 97 and very near to White's Creek. Major General Daniel Sickles' leg was amputated in the farm house and his wine was chilled in the farms well.

30. The George House is located at 237 Steinwehr Avenue and appears similar in construction to the Dobbin House. George George was its tenant in July 1863. It is thought to be the home where the body of Union General John Reynolds was taken on July 1.

31. It is a southern extension of Seminary Ridge, south of Pitzer Woods and the Millerstown Road. It intersects the Emmitsburg Road. Heavily wooded at the time of the battle, provided concealment for Hood's Division during the afternoon of July 2.

32. James Warfield's house, blacksmith shop and 13 acre farm is located on South Confederate Avenue and Millerstown Road. On July 2nd, General Barksdale and his Mississippi brigade briefly occupied the farm waiting for their orders to attack.

33. The headquarters marker for Hunt, who was the Chief of Artillery for the Army of the Potomac on Taneytown Road and just a bit south of the Leister House, which was Meade's headquarters.

34. The inscription is on one of the boulders in Devils Den. Tipton Station was trolley stop of the Gettysburg Electric Railway which took passengers to and from Crawford's Glen, Devil's Den and Tipton Park. The station was established during the 1894 construction of the trolley.

35. The site of the house is the southeast corner of the intersection of Chambersburg Street and West Street which is two blocks west of The Circle.

36. Gettysburg National Cemetery, Ohio Plot, Section C, Grave 4. His great grandson became president of the United States.

37. It was a wooden gate in a stone wall in the Abraham Trostle farmyard. Captain Bigelow, commander of the 9th Massachusetts. Bigelow posted his guns in the farmyard and upon the battery's forced retreat. The gate and stonewall impeded the battery's speedy withdrawl.

Gettysburg Campaign Exam Study Guide

QUESTIONS:

38. What is the Springs Hotel and where was it located?

39. What is 'Greene's Traverse'?

40. What is the 'Palmer Marker' and where is it located?

41. Where is the 'Heth Wounding Tree' site located?

42. Where is the 54th New York Volunteer Regiment's Skirmish Line marker located?

43. On Culp's Hill, where was the Iron Brigade located?

44. Where is Brigadier General Strong Vincent's wounding site?

Answers

38. The Gettysburg Springs Hotel was a post-war structure, a health water therapy and tourist site. The hotel was on the east side of Herr Ridge and quite near Willoughby Run. It was located near the Katalysine [Lithia] Springs and was built on the July 1 Confederate assault path to the McPherson Farm.

39. Ordered by Brigadier General George Greene, this particular fieldworks was built perpendicular to the saddle between Upper Culp's Hill and Lower Culp's Hill. The lower hill is about 400 yards south of the taller hill's crest. The earthworks were high enough for a man to kneel on the ground and fire over them. The traverse may have had a head log atop it.

40. On the morning of July 2, 1863, the 66th Ohio was moved to Culp's Hill and began constructing breastworks. The marker is on a rocky path on the east slope of Culp's Hill and not far from the large 66th Ohio monument. The marker is at the location where Major Joshua G. Palmer was mortally wounded. The marker rests on a knee-high, flat top boulder.

41. Major General Henry Heth was wounded on July 1, 1863 as he advanced with his troops through Herbst Woods located where the Herbst and McPherson farms meet. The tree marking the location where he was wounded has been cut down, but the stump remains at the north edge of the woods.

42. The advance marker for the 54th New York Infantry is located west of Rock Creek near Barlow Knoll. The marker is approximately 20 yards from the creek.

43. Regiments of the Iron Brigade occupied the peak of the Culp's Hill summit, facing northward and the other regiments falling in on the left. As a skirmish line, one company was placed at a right angle to the main line and faced Rock Creek.

44. There are two locations where eyewitnesses said he was wounded. One site has a marker on it; the second site has an inscription. The boulder with the monument to the 83rd Pennsylvania Volunteer Regiment has a figure that bears a striking resemblance to Vincent; but this is not recognized as a wounding site.

Gettysburg Campaign Exam Study Guide

QUESTIONS:

45. Where is there in Plum Run's valley between Devils Den and Little Round Top, a boulder with '40' and a diamond inscribed on it?

46. Where is a Parrott Rifled Canon No. 1 with the initials 'CP' stamped on it?

47. What is the location of Belmont Schoolhouse and what is its significance?

48. Where is the location and what is the significance of the wounding of Colonel Isaac Avery of the 6th North Carolina Volunteer Infantry?

49. Where is the location of Brigadier General Louis Armistead's death and where is his grave?

50. Where are the locations of the Heagy Farms?

Answers

45. The boulder is close to the 40th New York Monument near the park road bridge over Plum Run. The monument has a soldier on the ground, reclining into a stonewall and peering at Devils Den.

46. It is located in the town square of Hanover, Pennsylvania. It appears that the artillery tube is a reproduction as their weight, date of manufacture, and initials of the inspector are not on the muzzle. The muzzle opening is also not very "round." The letters "CP" on top of tube #1 may stand for either Commonwealth of Pennsylvania or City of Philadelphia. Alongside the artillery piece is another which is stamped No. 6.

47. The battle first shot occurred on Knoxlyn Ridge at Whistler's house and blacksmith shop. Like Whistler's residence Belmont School House was also on the north side of Chambersburg Pike. Both are east of Marsh Creek and west of Herr's Ridge.

48. He led a portion of the assault on East Cemetery Hill during the evening of July 2. Hays' Louisiana Tigers surging on his right. Near the beginning of the assault, Colonel Avery was shot in the neck and fell from his horse. He scribbled a note which he handed to a subordinate. The note read only, "Tell my father I died with my face to the enemy."

49. Armistead was wounded on the east side of the stonewall during the Grand Assault. He was taken to the 11th Corps field hospital at the George Spangler Farm where he died two days later. He is buried next to his uncle, Lieutenant Colonel George Armistead, commander of t Fort McHenry during the Battle of Baltimore during the War of 1812. Their graves are side-by-side at Old Saint Paul's Cemetery in Baltimore, Maryland.

50. The David Heagy farm with an orchard is on the north side of the Mummasburg Road and is associated with July 1 assault on the McClean Farmstead by the 45th New York and its support by Dilger's Ohio Battery. Another Heagy Farm is on the east side of the Emmitsburg Road and was the location of the step-off for the July 3rd cavalry assault by the 1st, 2nd, 5th U.S. Regular Army cavalry and the 6th Pennsylvania Volunteer cavalry on the far right of Longstreet's Corps.

Gettysburg Campaign Exam Study Guide

QUESTIONS:

51. What is the location and significance of the Adams County Alms Farm?

52. What is the location and significance of the Jacob Weikert Farm?

53. What is the location of Howe Avenue?

54. What is the location and significance of the Eagle Hotel?

55. What is the location and significance of Williams Avenue?

Answers

51. The Adams County Alms Farm is about 550 yards south of Blocher's/Barlow's Knoll. Barlow's Federal division passed over the farm during its advance and retreat on July 1. The graveyard of the alms farm is near the crest of Blocher's/Barlow's Knoll. The main building of the farm served as a temporary headquarters and observation post for Confederate corps commander Major General Richard Ewell. It also served as a Confederate field hospital. The buildings were removed during the mid-1900s and the Adams County Agriculture bureau's headquarters are now on the location.

52. Jacob Weikert owned 102 acres of land that included the east slope of Little Round Top. The house stands on the Taneytown Road and is approximately 650 years southeast of Little Round Top's crest. The Weikert family and Tillie Pierce fled the premises and then returned as the farm's building became a field hospital.

53. Howe Avenue is the extension of Wright Avenue when Wright Avenue crosses Taneytown Pike. Wright Avenue comes east off of the saddle between Big and Little Round Tops. Howe Avenue is less than a mile long, end in a cul-de-sac and on its north berm is the 119th Pennsylvania Volunteer Regiment's monument.

54. The Eagle Hotel was Brigadier General John Buford's headquarters during June 30-July 1. It opened for business in 1834 and was a large three story building which lasted until 1960. The hotel occupied the northeast corner of Chambersburg and Washington Streets. Today the location is occupied by a convenience store.

55. It is on upper Culp's Hill, connects Geary Avenue to Slocum Avenue at McKnight's/Steven's Knoll. On Williams Avenue there are no monuments.

Gettysburg Campaign Exam Study Guide

QUESTIONS:

56. What is the location and significance of Powers' Hill?

57. What is the location and significance of the artillery piece Ordnance Rifle numbered 233?

58. What is the location and significance of Berdan Avenue?

59. What is the location and significance of the Triangular Field?

60. What is the location and significance of the Pardee Field?

61. What is the location and significance of Sach's Bridge?

Answers

56. Powers Hill is located in the area of the Baltimore Pike, Granite Schoolhouse Lane, and Blacksmith Shop Road. Union artillery on Powers Hill shelled Confederates on Culp's Hill early in the morning of July 3, 1863. Right Wing Commander and Twelfth Corps Commander, Major-General Henry W. Slocum had his headquarters on at the base of the hill. The Federal Signal Corps had a station at the top of the hill. On July 3rd during the bombardment preceding Pickett's Charge Major-General George Meade temporarily moved his headquarters to Powers Hill.

57. The location of the piece is at the Brigadier General John Buford statue on the north side of the Chambersburg Road and across from the GNMP comfort and information station. It is believed to have fired the first Federal artillery round of the battle.

58. Berdan Avenue is less than ½ mile long and is on the west side of West Confederate Avenue. It marks the location of Pitzer's Woods and leads to three Federal monuments: Vermont Sharpshooters, New York Sharpshooters and the 3rd Maine Volunteer Regiment.

59. The field is adjacent to Devils Den on its west side and was the assault path of the 1st Texas and then Benning's brigade as it moved to the crest of Devils Den. The southwest corner of the field is a portion of the electric trolley line right of way.

60. The field is located on Geary Avenue at Culp s Hill. A large, flat rock with the inscription 'Pardee Field' etched upon it. Colonel Ario Pardee led the 147th Pennsylvania Infantry in an assault across open terrain and to drive the Confederates from fieldworks which were located behind a stone wall on the east side of this field.

61. It is a covered bridge over Marsh Creek, west of West Confederate Avenue. Millerstown Road runs past the bridge. The area around the bridge and the nearby Pitzer's Schoolhouse were locations of Confederate field hospitals.

Gettysburg Campaign Exam Study Guide

QUESTIONS:

62. What is the location and significance of the Emanuel Pitzer farm?

63. What is the location of the water pump at which Brigadier General Jubal Early wrote out the surrender terms for Gettysburg Borough on June 26th?

64. Where is the location of the furthest advanced marker of 1st Maryland [Confederate] Volunteer Infantry Regiment?

65. Where is the marked location of Major General Richard Ewell's headquarters?

66. Where is the marked location of Brigadier General Newton's headquarters?

67. Where is the location and significance of the death of Lieutenant Colonel Henry Fowler?

68. What is the location and significance of the Wentz House?

Answers

62. The Emanuel Pitzer Farm was west of West Confederate Avenue. During the morning of July 3 Pickett's Division crossed this farm enroute to Spangler's Woods. The Pitzer Farm became a field hospital for Pickett's Division. During the mid- 1950's Dwight Eisenhower purchased the farm and added it to the two other farms he owned.

63. The McClean House which is located at 11 Baltimore Street; it is on the west side of the street.

64. The marker over looks Pardee Field and quite close to Geary Avenue. It marks the regiment's advanced position in Pardee Field near the stonewall. Position marker is one foot square and is very weathered. The position marker is located little over 100 yards northwest of the main regimental monument.

65. The marker for Richard Ewell and the Second Army Corps is north of at the west intersection of the Mummasburg Road and the Eternal Peace Light Memorial driveway.

66. It is located on Pleasanton Avenue, west of the Taneytown Road and quite near the GNMP Grounds and Maintenance facility.

67. Fowler was promoted to Lieutenant Colonel of the 17th Connecticut soon after the Battle of Chancellorsville. In command of the regiment at Gettysburg, he was killed on July 1st by artillery fire. He rode a white horse to the crest of Blocher's/Barlow's Knoll and, within the sight of several witnesses he was decapitated by an artillery round. His body was never recovered.

68. The Wentz House was a one and a half story log house at the intersection of the Emmitsburg Road and the Wheatfield Road. It was a tenant house owned by Joseph Sherfy. The south side of the house faced the Peach Orchard. Thoughout the battle, John Wentz stayed in the houses basement.

Gettysburg Campaign Exam Study Guide

QUESTIONS:

69. What is the location and significance of the Rogers House?

70. What is the location and significance of Raffenberger's Hill?

71. Where is the location of the 'Killing Swale'?

72. Where is the location of the 'Spangler's Meadow?

73. What is the location of the capture of the 150th Pennsylvania's flag by the 14th North Carolina and how did the flag reappear?

74. What is the location of Chamberlain Avenue?

75. What is the location and significance of the 'Devils Slipper'?

76. Where are the 'Commonwealth of Pennsylvania' Parrott rifled cannon located?

Answers

69. The Peter Rogers home was on the west side of the Emmitsburg Road and to the north of the Klingel Farm buildings. The home was in the path of the Confederate assaults of July 2nd and 3rd. Josephine Miller, a close relative to Susan Rogers, stayed in the house throughout the battled; at times she cooked and baked for soldiers on both sides.

70. Raffenberger's Hill is the pre-battle name of East Cemetery Hill

71. The location is the upper reaches of Plum Run and east of the Klingle Farm and the Codori Farm buildings. Generally remembered for the number of killed, wounded and captured Federals in this area on July 2.

72. The meadow is at the eastern base of Culp's Hill. The meadow contains the Indiana State Memorial and was the site of the assault by the 2nd Massachusetts and 27th Indiana infantry regiments. It is believed that 8 color bearers of the 27th Indiana were killed or wounded in this meadow during the morning assault of July 3.

73. The flag was captured in the borough blocks of South Washington and West High Streets. The flag was in the baggage of Jefferson Davis in May 1865 near Irwinville, Georgia. It was returned to Pennsylvania in 1869.

74. Chamberlain Avenue no longer exists. It ran north to south on the east slope of Little Round Top. During the battle, it may have been a logging path on which the Pennsylvania Reserve regiments moved toward the 15th Alabama's assaults.

75. The Devils Slipper is on the west side of South Confederate Avenue is a large boulder which is generally considered to be cavalryman Brigadier General Elon Farnsworth's place of death during the late afternoon of July 3rd.

76. There are two 10 pound Parrott rifled cannons with the numbers 3 and 4 located on West Confederate Avenue past the South Carolina Monument.

235

Gettysburg Campaign Exam Study Guide

QUESTIONS:

77. What is the location of the only statue to a regimental commander on the battlefield and who does it honor?

78. What is the location of Cordori Spring and what is the significance?

79. Where is the location of the only original 6 pounder artillery piece on the battlefield?

80. What is the location and significance of 'Brockenborugh's Rock Quarry'?

81. What is the location and significance of the 5th Ohio's skirmish line 'headquarters'?

82. What is the location of the Wible Quarry and what is it significance?

83. What is the significance of McGilvery Avenue?

84. What is Red Patch?

Answers

77. The monument to William Wells is on South Confederate Avenue. Wells was a major in the First Vermont Cavalry Regiment and he led a battalion of the First Vermont Cavalry during Farnsworth's charge on July 3rd.

78. The spring was on Cemetery Ridge, northwest of the Pennsylvania Memorial and very near of the intersection of Hancock and Pleasonton Avenues. It was developed by the trolley line as a stop in its tour.

79. It is located at the intersection of Emmitsburg Road and South Confederate Avenue. It is a part of the monument to the Branch Artillery which was commanded by Captain Alexander C. Latham. The piece is pointed toward the Round Tops.

80. It is located on the west slope of McPherson's Ridge. On the south side of the rock quarry is Herbst's Wood Lot. During its July 1st assault it forced Brockenbrough's Brigade to its left and toward the Emmitsburg Road.

81. The location of the skirmish line marker is on Geary Avenue and very close to Pardee Field.

82. It is a quarry dug after the battle located in Rose's Woods just south of the sharp bend in Brooke Avenue. Decades after the battle, the Rose Farm was owned by William Wible. He created the quarry to provide granite for flank markers, monument bases.

83. McGilvery Artillery Avenue was a south bound route on the Gettysburg Electric Railway. McGilvery Artillery Avenue has a cast iron tablet which was made and set in 1896, removed 1974 and restored in 1992 and set again in place. The location is on south side of Wheatfield Road, near Birney Avenue.

84. Red Patch is a summer home built after the war by Union Brevet Major General Charles Collis. It is located on West Confederate Avenue and today is a private residence. The home's name, Red Patch, relates to the Union 3rd Army Corps' uniform patch which is a red Maltese Cross.

Gettysburg Campaign Exam Study Guide

QUESTIONS:

85. Who is Herman Haupt and what is the location of his home in Gettysburg?

86. What is the location and significance of Josiah Benner's springhouse?

87. What is the location of the 123rd New York regiment's skirmish and what is its significance?

88. Where is Slocum's headquarters marker located?

89. Is there a second Spangler's Spring?

90. What is the location of the Army of the Potomac's right flank marker?

Answers

85. Haupt was a civil engineer, a railroad construction engineer. During the war he was a Federal Army general and revolutionized military logistics and transportation. From 1840 to 1847, Haupt was a professor of mathematics and engineering at Pennsylvania College. He designed and built a house which he name "Oakridge". The house served both Federals and Confederates a field hospital. It still stands on the southeast corner of West Confederate Ave and the Fairfield Road.

86. The Josiah Benner House in Straban Township an is readily viewed from Blocher's/Barlow's Barlow's. The farmhouse predates the battle. The farm's location on Old Harrisburg Road placed it on the assault path of Early's division on the afternoon of July 1. The one-story springhouse just east of the farmhouse was likely used as a temporary cover for skirmishers of both armies and would have provided water and provided cool storage of food for wounded soldiers in the hospitals of the Benner house and barn.

87. The position marker indicates skirmish line afternoon July 3; it is in the about 300 feet east of 123rd New York's Culp's Hill monument on south Slocum Avenue. The marker is about 1 foot by 2 feet and on its top is inscribed a star.

88. It is located on located on Powers Hill.

89. There is the granite encased Spangler's Spring in Spangler's Meadow and there is a second Spangler's Spring about 200 yards uphill between the upper and lower Culp's Hill.

90. The position marker for the right flank is southeast of Gettysburg and on Neil Avenue, which is frequently called "Lost Lane" because of its remoteness. On July 3 Neill's Brigade of the Sixth Army Corps was ordered to protect the Army of the Potomac's main supply line on Baltimore Pike. The position marker is near the monument to the 61st Pennsylvania Infantry, which was the right flank of the brigade.

QUESTIONS:

91. What is the location of Wesley Culp's grave?

92. In Evergreen Cemetery, which section holds the remains of those killed during the battle?

93. What is the location of the 26th Pennsylvania Emergency Regiment's "Action" Marker?

94. What is the location of Blocher's Knoll?

95. What is the location of the original advance marker of the 27th Connecticut?

96. What is the location of Samuel Crawford's headquarters during the night of July 2-July 3?

97. State the name of the last Civil War veteran to serve as the Gettysburg National Military Park superintendent.

98. Which Pennsylvania [Gettysburg] College professor kept accurate descriptions of the weather conditions during the Gettysburg Campaign?

Things Licensed Battlefield Guides Know

ANSWERS

91. Wesley Culp's body was never recovered. Speculations include: his body was recovered and buried [unmarked] in the family plot of Evergreen Cemetery; it may still be buried somewhere on Culp's Hill; his remains were reinterred in a southern cemetery after the war and listed as unknown; his relatives retrieved his body and buried in the basement of the Culp's farmhouse.

92. Section C

93. It is at the intersection of Chambersburg, West, Spring and Buford Streets.

94. Blocher's Knoll is also known as Barlow's Knoll. The Josiah Benner farm and the Old Harrisburg Road may be view when looking northeast

95. The location is close to Brooke Avenue; the large monument to the 27th Connecticut is in the Wheatfield.

96. On the northeast slope of Little Round Top.

97. Lieutenant Colonel Emmor B. Cope. Cope was the last Civil War veteran to be a Superintendent of Gettysburg National Military Park.

98. Dr. Michael Jacobs, a math professor

Section Thirty-Eight
Final Monuments

"Northwest elevations of 13th Massachusetts monument, Robinson Avenue, Tipton #875 (c. 1887)" Tipton DS #5033

Gettysburg Campaign Exam Study Guide

Final Monuments

1. Spangler Spring [intersection of Geary, Slocum and Carmen Avenues]

2. Pennsylvania Light Artillery [Knapp's Battery] [atop Powers' Hill on Granite School House Road]

3. 7th Maine Volunteer Infantry [Neill Avenue]

4. Hancock-Armistead Memorial, George Spangler Farm, [Blacksmith Shop Road]

5. 6th Maine Volunteer Infantry [Howe Avenue]

6. 5th Wisconsin Volunteer Infantry [Howe Avenue]

7. 119th Pennsylvania [Howe Avenue]

8. 5th Maine Battery [Steven's], McKnight Knoll on Slocum Avenue

9. 46th Pennsylvania Volunteer Infantry, Colgrove Avenue

Gettysburg Campaign Exam Study Guide

Final Monuments

1. 29th Ohio Volunteer Infantry, Slocum Avenue

2. 1st Maryland Cavalry, East Cavalry Battlefield

3. David Gregg Memorial Shaft, East Cavalry Battlefield

4. 3rd Pennsylvania Cavalry, East Cavalry Battlefield

5. Michigan Cavalry Brigade 1st, 5th, 6th & 7th Michigan Cavalry [Wolverine Brigade] East Cavalry Battlefield

6. 1st New Jersey Volunteer Cavalry, East Cavalry Battlefield

7. 1st Maine Cavalry, East Cavalry Battlefield

8. 3rd Pennsylvania Volunteer Artillery, Battery H, East Cavalry Battlefield

9. 10th New York Cavalry, East Cavalry Battlefield

Gettysburg Campaign Exam Study Guide

248

Final Monuments

1. 6th Pennsylvania Volunteer Cavalry, South Cavalry Battlefield

2. 105th Pennsylvania Volunteer Infantry, Emmitsburg Road

3. 73rd New York Volunteer Infantry, Excelsior Field

4. Brigadier General James Johnston Pettigrew, death site, Bunker Hill, West Virginia

5. Company A, Purnell Legion (Maryland) Cavalry

6. 105th Pennsylvania Volunteer Infantry, emblem centerpiece, Emmitsburg Road

7. 5th Pennsylvania Reserves Volunteer Infantry, crest of Big Round Top

8. 12th Pennsylvania Reserves Volunteer Infantry, crest of Big Round Top

9. 9th Pennsylvania Reserves Volunteer Infantry, 9th Pennsylvania Reserves, base of Little Round Top near the intersection of Warren and Sykes Avenues.

Gettysburg Campaign Exam Study Guide

10. 6th Pennsylvania Reserves Volunteer Infantry, Wheatfield Avenue
11. 11th Pennsylvania Reserves Volunteer Infantry, Ayers Avenue
12. 2nd Pennsylvania Reserves Volunteer Infantry, Ayers Avenue
13. 1st Pennsylvania Reserves Volunteer Infantry, Ayers Avenue
14. 10th Pennsylvania Reserves Volunteer Infantry, South Confederate Avenue
15. New Jersey Brigade: 1st, 2nd, 3rd, 4th & 15th Infantry; east side of Sedgwick Avenue south of the intersection with United States Avenue.
16. 13th Pennsylvania Reserves, Houck's Ridge

Bibliography of Works Consulted for Volumes One and Two

Atlases and Maps

The Battlefield at Gettysburg, Thomas A. Desjardin, FNPG, 1998.

Gettysburg: A Battlefield Atlas, Craig L. Symonds, Nautical and Aviation Publishing, 1992.

Gettysburg Battlefield, Gettysburg, Pennsylvania, 1863, McElfresh Map Company LLC., 1997.

Gettysburg Battlefield, Gettysburg, Pennsylvania, 1863, McElfresh Map Company LLC., 2007.

Gettysburg Campaign Atlas, Philip Laino, Gatehouse Press, 2009.

Gettysburg National Military Park, Pennsylvania: Civil War Battle Series, Trailhead Graphics, 2000.

Gettysburg: Invasion and Retreat, Maryland Civil War Trails, 2007.

Haldesperson's Civil War Maps, www.posix.com/CWmaps

The Maps of Gettysburg: An Atlas of the Gettysburg Campaign, June 3-July 13, 1863. Bradley Gottfried, Savas Beatie, LLL, 2010.

The Official Military Atlas of the Civil War, Major George B. Davis et al., Barnes and Noble Books, Inc., 2003.

A Theatre Map of the Gettysburg Campaign 1863, Earl McElfresh, 2003.

The West Point Atlas of the American Civil War, U.S.M.A. Department of History, West Point 1978.

Books, Seminar Papers, and Theses

The Campaign of Gettysburg: Command Decisions, Lieutenant Colonel William D. Hewitt, 2012

After July: The Effects of the Battle of Gettysburg, Marilyn Browfield Rudasky, Masters Thesis, Youngstown State University, 1979.

The American Civil War in 1863: Programs of the Eighth GNMP Seminar, Gettysburg National Military Park, 2001.

American Heritage History of the Battle of Gettysburg, Craig L. Symonds, Harper Collins, Inc, 2001.

Artifacts Donated to GNMP by the FNPG, Denise Carper, FNPG Inc., 2001,

Bibliography of Works Consulted for Volumes One and Two

The Artillery of Gettysburg, Bradley M. Gottfried, Cumberland House. 2008.

The Attack and Defense of Little Round Top, Oliver Wilcox Norton, Morningside House Inc., 1978.

Battle for the Barb: The Attack and Defense of Culp's Hill on July 2, 1863, Charles C. Fennell, FNPG, Inc., 2001.

The Battle of Gettysburg, Harry Pfanz and Scott Hartwig, Eastern National Inc., 1994.

Battles and Leaders of the Civil War, Buell and Johnson, Thomas Yoseloff Inc., 1967.

Beneath a Northern Sky: A Short History of the Gettysburg Campaign, Steven E. Woodworth, Scholarly Resources, Inc., 2003.

Beyond the Gatehouse: Gettysburg's Evergreen Cemetery, Brian A. Kennell, Evergreen Cemetery Association, 2000.

Brave and Stubborn Resistance: The 73rd Pennsylvania and Cemetery Hill, Renae Maclachlan, FNPG, 2003.

Brigades of Gettysburg The Union and Confederate Brigades at the Battle of Gettysburg, Bradley M. Gottfried, DaCapo Press, 2002.

Campaign and Battle of Gettysburg, E. J. Fieberger, Bloodstone Press, 1984.

Cordori Family and Farm, Pam Newhouse, FNPG Inc., 1999.

Colors of Courage: Gettysburg's Forgotten History of Immigrants, Women, and African Americans in the Civil Wars Defining Battle, Margaret S. Creighton, Basic Books Inc, 2005.

Command and Communication Frictions in the Gettysburg Campaign, Philip M. Cole, Colecraft Industries, 2006.

Brave and Stubborn Resistance: The 73rd Pennsylvania and Cemetery Hill, Renae Maclachlan, FNPG, 2003.

Brigades of Gettysburg The Union and Confederate Brigades at the Battle of Gettysburg, Bradley M. Gottfried, DaCapo Press, 2002.

Campaign and Battle of Gettysburg, E. J. Fieberger, Bloodstone Press, 1984.

Cordori Family and Farm, Pam Newhouse, FNPG Inc., 1999.

Colors of Courage: Gettysburg's Forgotten History of Immigrants, Women, and African Americans in the Civil Wars Defining Battle, Margaret S. Creighton, Basic Books Inc, 2005.

Command and Communication Frictions in the Gettysburg Campaign, Philip M. Cole, Colecraft Industries, 2006.

Brave and Stubborn Resistance: The 73rd Pennsylvania and Cemetery Hill, Renae Maclachlan, FNPG, 2003.

Brigades of Gettysburg The Union and Confederate Brigades at the Battle of Gettysburg, Bradley M. Gottfried, DaCapo Press, 2002.

Campaign and Battle of Gettysburg, E. J. Fieberger, Bloodstone Press, 1984.

Cordori Family and Farm, Pam Newhouse, FNPG Inc., 1999.

Colors of Courage: Gettysburg's Forgotten History of Immigrants, Women, and African Americans in the Civil Wars Defining Battle, Margaret S. Creighton, Basic Books Inc, 2005.

Command and Communication Frictions in the Gettysburg Campaign, Philip M. Cole, Colecraft Industries 2006.

The Complete Gettysburg Guide, J. David Petruzzi and Steven Stanley, Savas Beattie, 2009.

Concise Guide to the Artillery at Gettysburg, Gregory A. Coco, Thomas Publications, 1998.

Confederate Monuments at Gettysburg, David G. Martin, Combined Books, Inc., 1986.

Crossroads of the Conflict: Defining Hours for the Blue and Gray: A Guide to the Monuments of Gettysburg, Donald W. McLaughlin, Outskirts Press, 2008.

Culp's Hill at Gettysburg: The Mountain Trembled, John M. Archer, Thomas Publications, 2002.

Days of Darkness: Gettysburg Civilians, William G. Williams, Berkley Press, 1986.

Days of Uncertainty and Dread: The Ordeal Endured by the Citizens at Gettysburg, Gerald R. Bennett, Plank Suburban Press, 1994.

Debris of Battle: The Wounded of Gettysburg, Gerard A. Patterson, Stackpole Books, 1997.

Decisions at Gettysburg: Nineteen Critical Decisions that Defined the Campaign, Matt Spruill, University of Tennessee Press, 2011.

Devil's Den: A History and Guide, Garry E. Adelman and Timothy H. Smith, Thomas Publications, 1997.

Defeating Lee: A History of the Second Army Corps, Army of the Potomac, Lawrence A. Kreiser, Jr., Indiana University Press, 2011.

Bibliography of Works Consulted for Volumes One and Two

Double Canister at Ten Yards: Federal Artillery and the Repulse of Pickett's Charge, David Schultz, Rank and File Publications, 1995.

Early Photography at Gettysburg, William A. Fassanito, Thomas Publications, 1995.

Encounter at Cemetery Hill: The Vision-Place of Souls, Denise Doyle Killmeyer, FNPG Inc., 2003.

Ewell's Approach: A Circumstance Dictated, Wayne Wachsmuth, FNPG, Inc., 1998.

Farms at Gettysburg: The Fields of Battle, Timothy H. Smith, Thomas Publications, 2007.

A Feat of Arms: Freeman McGilvery and the Plum Run Line, Renae MacLachlan, FNPG, Inc., 2003.

Fields of Glory: The Facts Book of the Battle of Gettysburg, Herbert O Brown and Dwight V. Nitz, Thomas Publications, 1990.

Firestorm at Gettysburg: Civilian Voices, June –Novmeber 1863

Jim Slade and John Alexander, Schiffer Military History, 1998.

The First Day at Gettysburg: Essays on Confederate and Union Leadership, Gary Gallagher, Editor, Kent State University Press, 1992.

First Day at Gettysburg: A Walking Tour, James E. Thomas, Thomas Publications, 2005.

Flames Beyond Gettysburg: The Confederate Expedition to the Susquehanna River, June 1863, Scott L. Mingus, Sr., Savas Beattie LLC., 2011.

The Fog Of Gettysburg: The Myths and Mysteries of the Battle, Ken Allers, Sr., Cumberland House, 2008

Forward and On We Went: Eighth Louisiana's Twilight Assault on Cemetery Hill, Renae MacLachlan, FNPG Inc., 2003.

Generals of Gettysburg: Leaders of America's Greatest Battle, Larry Tagg, DaCapo Press, 1998.

Generation on the March: The Union Army at Gettysburg, Edmund J. Raus, Jr., Thomas Publications, 1996.

Geology and the Gettysburg Campaign, Andrew Brown, Pennsylvania State Geological Survey, 1962.

Gettysburg, Stephen W. Sears, Houghton Mifflin Company, 2003.

Gettysburg Battle Lands: FNPG Land Purchases for the GNMP, Charles C. Fenell, Jr., FNPG Inc, 1999.

The Gettysburg Campaign: A Study in Command, Edwin B. Coddington, Scribner's Publishing, 1968.

The Gettysburg Campaign and the First Day of Battle: Programs of the Tenth GNMP Seminar, Gettysburg National Military Park, 2005.

Gettysburg: The Complete Pictorial Guide of the Battlefield Monuments, D. Scott Hartwig and Ann Marie Hartwig, Thomas Publications, 1995.

Gettysburg: Culp's and Cemetery Hill, Harry W. Pfanz, University of North Carolina Press, 1993.

Gettysburg Day Three, Jeffry D. Wert, Simon and Schuster, Inc, 2001.

Gettysburg Farmstead Guide, Denise Carper and Renae Hardoby, Friends of the National Parks at Gettysburg, 2000.

Gettysburg: A Journey in Time, William A. Frassnito, Scribners Inc., 1975.

The Gettysburg Nobody Knows, Gabor S. Boritt, editor, Oxford University Press, 1997.

Gettysburg: The First Day, Harry W. Pfanz, University of North Carolina Press, 2001.

Gettysburg: The Second Day, Harry W. Pfanz, University of North Carolina Press, 1987.

Gettysburg: A Testing of Courage, Noah Andre Trudeu, Harper Collins Inc., 2002.

Gettysburg July 1, Completely Revised Second Edition, David G. Martin, Combined Books, 1996.

Gettysburg 1 July 1863: Confederate: The Army of Northern Virginia, Order of Battle Series, James Arnold and Roberta Weiner, Osprey Military Publishing, 1998.

Gettysburg for Walkers Only, Jerome H. Miller and Dolores E. Miller, Thomas Publications, 1991.

Gettysburg Heroes: Perfect Soldiers, Ground, Glenn W. LaFantasie, Indiana University Press

Gettysburg Hour by Hour: An Account of the Battle, Harry Roach, Thomas Publications, 1993.

Gettysburg's Bloody Wheatfield, Jay Jorgensen, White Mane Press, 2001.

Gettysburg's Confederate Dead, Gregory A. Coco, Thomas Publications, 2003.

Gettysburg: Confederate High Tide, Thomas A. Lewis et al., Time Life Inc., 1985.

Gettysburg: Memory, Market and American Shrine, Jim Weeks, Princeton University Press, 2003.

Gettysburg Seminary's Role in a Defining Event in American History, Frederick K. Wentz, Gettysburg Lutheran Seminary, n.d.

Gettysburg: The Souvenir Guide to the National Military Park, James Gross and Andre Collins, Gross & Collins copyright, 1971.

Gettysburg: Stories of Men and Monuments As Told By The Battlefield Guides, Frederick W. Hawthorne, Association of Licensed Gettysburg Battlefield Guides, Inc., 1988.

Gettysburg Then and Now: Touring the Battlefield with World Photos, 1863-1889, William A. Frassnito, Thomas Publications, 1996.

Gettysburg Then and Now Companion, William A. Frassnito, Thomas Publications, 1997.

Grappling with Death: The Union Second Corps Hospital at Gettysburg, Roland R. Maust, Morningside House, 2001.

Guide to The Battle Of Gettysburg, Jay Luvass and Harold W. Nelson, University of Kansas Press, 1994.

Guide to Pennsylvania Troops At Gettysburg, Richard Rollins and David Schultz, Rank and File Publications, 1996.

Here Come The Rebels!, Wilbur S. Nye, Morningside House, 1994.

High Tide at Gettysburg, Glenn Tucker, Bobbs-Merrill Inc., 1958.

High Water Mark: The Army of Northern Virginia in the Gettysburg Campaign, Programs of the Seventh Annual Gettysburg Seminar,

The Hour Was One of Horror: East Cemetery Hill at Gettysburg, John M. Archer, Thomas Publications, 1997.

Human Interest Stories of the Gettysburg Campaign, Volumes I and II, Scott Mingus, Sr., Colecraft Industries, 2006 and 2007

The Great Invasion, Jacob Hoke, Stan Clark Military Books, 1992.

The Hospital on Seminary Ridge at the Battle of Gettysburg, Michael A.

Dreese, McFarland and Company, 2002.

Inscription at Gettysburg: In Memoriam to Captain David Acheson, Company C, 140th Pennsylvania Volunteers, Sara Gould Walters, Thomas Publications, 1991.

In The Eye of the Storm: The Farnsworth House and the Battle of Gettysburg, Timothy H. Smith, Farnsworth Military Impressions, 2008.

Into The Fight: Pickett's Charge at Gettysburg, John Michael Priest, White Mane Press, 1998.

Isn't This Glorious!: the 15th, 19th, and 20 Massachusetts Volunteer Infantry Regiments at Gettysburg's Copse of Trees, Edwin R. Root and Jeffery D. Stocker, Moon Trail Books Inc., 2006.

The Gettysburg Campaign, June-July 1863, Carol Reardon and Tom Vossler, 2013.

A Field Guide To Gettysburg, Carol Reardon and Tom Vossler.

The Pennsylvania Reserves In The Civil War, Uzal W. Ent, 2014.

Kelly's Heroes: The Irish Brigade at Gettysburg, T. L.Murphy, Farnsworth House Publications, 1997.

Killed in Action: Eyewitness Accounts of the Last Moments of 100 Union Soldiers Who Died at Gettysburg, Gregory A. Coco, Thomas Publications, 1992.

The Last Stand of the U.S. Army at Gettysburg, Jeffrey C. Hall, Indiana University Press, 2003.

Leadership in the Campaign and Battle of Gettysburg, Papers of the Ninth Gettysburg National Military Park Seminar, 2002.

Learning the Battle of Gettysburg: A Guide to the Official Records, BenjaminY. Dixon, Thomas Publications, 2007.

Lee and Longstreet at Gettysburg, Glenn Tucker, Bobbs-Merrill Inc., 1968.

Legends of Gettysburg: Separating Fact From Fiction, Thomas A. Desjardins, FNGP, Inc., 1996.

A Lion To The Last: Lt. William J. Fisher and the 10th U.S. Infantry, Renae MacLaughlin, FNPG Inc, 2003.

Little Round Top: A Detailed Tour Guide, Garry E. Adelman, Thomas Publications, 2000.

Bibliography of Works Consulted for Volumes One and Two

The Location of the Monuments, Markers and Tablets on Gettysburg Battlefield, Kathy George Harrison, Thomas Publications, 1993.

The Louisiana Tigers in the Gettysburg Campaign, June-July 1863, Scott L. Mingus, Louisiana State University Press, 2009.

Meade of Gettysburg, Freeman Cleaves, Morningside House, Inc., 1980.

The Medal of Honor At Gettysburg, B. T. Arrington, Thomas Publications, 1996.

Morning at Willoughby Run: The Morning Battle at Gettysburg, July 1, 1863, Richard S. Shue, Thomas Publications Inc., 1998.

Most Promising Young Man of the South: James Johnston Pettigrew and His Men at Gettysburg, Clyde N. Wilson, McWhiney Foundation Press, 1998.

The Most Shocking Battle I Have Witnessed: The Second Day At Gettysburg, Programs of the 2006 GNMP Seminar, Gettysburg National Military Park, 2008.

Mr. Lincoln's Army: The Army Of the Potomac In The Gettysburg Campaign, Programs of the Sixth Annual GNMP Seminar, Gettysburg National Military Park, 1997.

My Gettysburg Battle Experiences, Captain George Hillyer, 9th Georgia Infantry, CSA, Gregory A. Coco, Thomas Publications, 2005.

Never Desert the Old Flag: 50 Stories of Union Battle Flags and Color-Bearers at Gettysburg, Michael Dreese, Thomas Publications, 2002.

Nine Months to Gettysburg: Stannard's Vermonters and the Repulse of Pickett's Charge, Howard Coffin, Countryman Press, 1997.

Nothing But Glory: Pickett's Division at Gettysburg, Kathy Georg Harrison, Thomas Publications, 2001.

One Continuous Fight: The Retreat rom Gettysburg and the Pursuit of Lee's Army of Northern Virginia, July 4-14, 1863, Eric J. Wittenberg, J. David Petruzzi, and Michael F. Nugent, Savas Beatie, Inc., 2008.

Our Bravest and B est: The Iron Brigade at Gettysburg, Renae McLachlan, FNPG, Inc., 2001.

Plenty of Blame To Go Around: Jeb Stuart's Controversial Ride to Gettysburg, Eric J. Wittenberg and J. David Petruzzi, Savas Beatie LLC., 2009.

Pickett's Charge! Eyewitness Accounts, Richard Rollins, editor, Rank and

File Publications, 1994.

Pickett's Charge: The Last Attack at Gettysburg, Earl J. Hess, University of North Carolina Press, 2001.

Regimental Strengths and Loses at Gettysburg, Fourth Edition, John W. Busey and David G. Martin, Longstreet House Inc., 2005.

Remaking of the Gettysburg Battlefield Five Times Over!, Benjamin Y. Dixon, Adams Seminar, Friends of the Gettysburg Battlefield, 2008.

Retreat From Gettysburg: Lee, Logistics and the Pennsylvania Campaign, Kent Masterson Brown, University of North Carolina Press, 2005.

Sanctuary For The Wounded: The Civil War Hospital at Christ Lutheran Church, Gettysburg, Pennsylvania, Christ Evangelical Lutheran Church, 2010.

The Second Day At Gettysburg,: Essays On Confederate and Union Leadership, Gary Gallagher, Editor, Kent State University Press, 1993.

The Shriver's Story: Eyewitnesses To The Battle Of Gettysburg, Nancie W. Gudmestad, Shriver House Museum, 2008.

Sickles At Gettysburg, James A. Hessler, Savas Beatie, LLC. 2009.

Silent Sentinals: A Reference Guide To The Artillery At Gettysburg, George W. Newton, Savas Beatie Inc., 2005.

Small Arms at Gettysburg" Infantry and Cavalry Weapons In America's Greatest Battle, Joseph G. Bilby, Westholme Publishing Inc., 2008.

Soldiers' National Cemetery, Revised Report, n.a., Thomas Publications, 1988.

Stand Firm Ye Boys From Maine: The 20th Maine and the Gettysburg Campaign, Thomas A. Desjardin, Oxford University Press, 1995.

Stone's Brigade and the Fight for McPherson's Farm: Battle of Gettysburg July 1 1863, James J. Dougherty, Combined Publishing, 2001.

The Story of Lee's Headquarters, Gettysburg, Pennsylvania, Timothy H. Smith, Thomas Publications, 1995.

Strange and Blighted Land: Gettysburg, The Aftermath of a Battle, Gregory A. Coco, Thomas Publications, 1995.

Summer Thunder: A Battlefield Guide to the Artillery at Gettysburg, Matt Spruill, University of Tennessee Press, 2010.

Sword of Lincoln: The Army of the Potomac, Jeffry D. Wert, Simon and

Schuster, 2005.

Their Silent Vigil: A Complete Guide to the Monuments of the Gettysburg National Military Park, Volume I, Robert J. Nixon, Tate Publishing & Enterprises, 2009.

These Honored Dead: How the Story of Gettysburg Shaped American Memory, Thomas A. Desjardins, DaCapo Press, 2003.

They Saved Little Round Top, Gettysburg July 2, 1863, Ken Discorfano, Thomas Publications, 2002.

"They Will Remember Gettysburg": The Rupp Family, House and Tannery, Emma K. Young, FNPG, Inc., 2002.

Third Day at Gettysburg and Beyond, Gary Gallagher, editor, University of North Carolina Press, 1994.

The Third Day: The Fate of the Nation, July 3, 1863, 2008 GNMP Seminar, Gettysburg National Military Park, 2010.

This Flag Never Goes Down: 40 Stories of Confederate Battle Flags and Color Bears at Gettysburg, Michael Dreese, Thomas Publications, 2004.

This Is Holy Ground: A History of the Gettysburg Battlefield, Barbara L. Platt, Huggins Printing, 2001.

Those Damned Black Hats! The Iron Brigade in the Gettysburg Campaign, Lance J. Herdegen, Savas Beatie LLC, 2008.

Those Damned Red Flags of the Rebellion: The Confederate Battle Flag at Gettysburg, Richard Rollins, Rank and File Publications, 1997.

Torn Families: Death and Kinship at the Battle of Gettysburg, Michael A. Dreese, McFarland and Company, 2007.

Trust in God and Fear Nothing: General Lewis A. Armistead, CSA, Wayne E. Motts, Farnsworth House Military House Impressions, 1994.

Twilight at Little Round Top: July 2 1863, The Tide Turns at Gettysburg, Glenn W. LaFantasie, John Wiley and Sons, Inc., 2005

A Vast Sea of Misery: A History and Guide to the Unon and Confederate Field Hospitals at Gettysburg, July 1-November 20, 1863, Second Edition, Gregory A. Coco, Thomas Publications, 1992.

War Of The Rebellion Official Record of the Union and Confederate Armies, Series I, Vol. 27, Parts I, II, III, National Historical Society, 1971.

War Stories: A Collection of 150 Little Know Human Interest Accounts of the Campaign and the Battle of Gettysburg, Gregory A. Coco, Thomas

Publications, 1992.

Wasted Valor: Confederate Dead At Gettysburg, Gregory Coco, Thomas Publications, 1990.

The Wheatfield at Gettysburg: A Walking Tour, Jay Jorgensen, Thomas Publications, 2002.

When the Smoke Cleared at Gettysburg: The Tragic Aftermath of the Bloodiest Battle of the Civil War, George Sheldon, Cumberland House, 2003.

Winfield Scott Hancock, Gettysburg Hero, Perry D. Jamieson, McWhiney Foundation Press, 2004.

Witness to Gettysburg, Richard Wheeler, Blue and Grey Press, 1994.

Women at Gettysburg, 1863, E F. Conklin, Thomas Publications, 1993.

The World Will Long Remember, JoAnna M. McDonald, White Mane Publishing Company, 1996.

Yellow Hill: Reconstructing the Past Puzzle of the Lost Community at Yellow Hill, Debra Sandoe McCauslin, For The Cause Publications, 2007.

Websites

Associations of Licensed Battlefield Guides, www.gettysburgtourguides.org.

Gettysburg Daily, Gettysburg Licensed Battlefield Guides, www.gettysburgdaily.com

Gettysburg Discussion Group Online, http://www.gdg.org/

Hal Jesperson's Civil War Maps, www.posix.com/CWmaps

McAllister Mill Underground Railroad Site online, Dean Schultz, http://www.gdg.org/Research/Underground%20Railroad/mill.htm

Stone Sentinels: Battlefield Monuments of the Civil War, Steve Hawks,http://www.stonesentinels.com/

Virtual Tour: The Story of the Battle of Gettysburg, Gettysburg National Military Park,www.nps.gov/gett

Compact Discs

The Complete Gettysburg Guide, Volume One: The Battlefield, J. David

Stanley and Steven Stanley, 2010.

The Gettysburg Park Commission Photos: Then and Now, Garry E. Adelman, Gettysburg Discussion Group edition, 2007.

Monumental Battlefields: Monuments and Markers at Gettysburg, n.a., Civil War Software, 2002.

Virtual Gettysburg, Stephen Recker, Another Software Miracle, 2005.

Magazines and Seminar Handouts

America's Civil War, Issues 9:3, 12:3, 12:4, 13:3, 14:3, 15:3,17:6, 18:4, 20:3, 22:2,

Blue & Gray: For Those Who Still Hear The Guns, Blue & Gray Inc., Special Issues

12:3,12:6,14:5, 15:5,16:5, 17:5,19:2, 21:1, 22:2, 23:1, 24:2, 25:3, 28:4

Blue and Gray Sea of Misery: Civil War Hospital Sites, George Spangler Farm, Eleventh Corps Hospital and Camp Letterman, Phil Lechak, 13th Biennial Seminar, 2010.

Civil War Regiments, A Journal of the American Civil War, 6:3, Gettysburg Regimental Leadership and Command, Savas Publishing, 1992.

Civil War Times Magazine, Issues 37:4, 46:5, 47:2,

Gettysburg Commemorative Issue, Prime Media, 2003.

Gettysburg Compiler, 125th Commemorative Edition, Fiftieth Anniversary Rededication of The Eternal Light Peace Memorial, Jerold Wikoff, ed., Times & News Publishing Company, 1988.

Gettysburg Magazine, Numbers 1 through 51.

Military Geology at the Battle of Gettysburg, July 1863, Peter Doyle, Geology Today, 22: 4

North And South Magazine, Issues 1:3, 1:6, 2:2, 2:5, 2:7, 3:2, 3:3,3:4, 4:3, 4:5, 4:7, 5:4, 5:5, 5:6, 6:5, 7:7, 8:1, 8:4, 9:1, 9:6,

Made in United States
North Haven, CT
10 February 2025